# THE SPATULATTA COOKBOOK

by Isabella and
Olivia Gerasole

Recipes for kids, by kids, from the James Beard
award-winning Spatulatta Web site

📖 **SCHOLASTIC**

**Photographs by John Zich/zrimages.com**
**www.spatulatta.com**

## ACKNOWLEDGEMENTS

We want to say thanks to all the people who have helped us make Spatulatta and this cookbook a reality. Our mom, Heidi Umbhau, for her creativity and for always supporting us; our webcast producer Gaylon Emerzian for her hours and hours of work behind the scenes and always making it fun for us. And the men in our lives: our pop, Vince Gerasole, for passing down his family's recipes and stories, and loving everything we made, even the mud pies. Mr. Roger Brown for dashing up the street with last-minute ingredients, and Mr. John Scott, our videotape editor, who watches us cooking for hours on end and never gets a bite.

Thanks to the people who shared their recipes with us: Gary, Sona, Nicky and Andrew Rejebian, Sabrina, Cody, and Taylor Harrell and their mom Stevie; Peter and Dianne Cotsirilos, Janie Herbener; Maggie, Brendan and Gannon Leech; Broderick Kelley; Lisa Reitman, Marcia Streicher from Petit Chefs, Karen Duffin from the Happy Tart and Chef Jorge from That Little Mexican Café in Evanston. And to Aunt Kate for all her help.

A huge thanks to Crate and Barrel for their generous support; our editor Brenda Murray and the talented team at Scholastic. And the other members of the Spatulatta Cookbook team: Doe Coover, Karen Levin, and the fabulous Mr. John Zich.

Library of Congress Cataloging-in-Publication Data available

ISBN 13: 978-0-439-02250-7
ISBN 10: 0-439-02250-9

10 9 8 7 6 5 4 3 2 1          07 08 09 10 11

Printed in China
First printing, September 2007
Book design by CALICO www.calico-kids.com
Photo credits: Pages 10-11: © PHOTOS.com, © STOCKDISC CLASSIC/ALAMY, iStockPhoto.com.

# CONTENTS

Cooking has been part of our lives for as long as we can remember. We're Italian! For big parties, we helped our pop make homemade pasta with his Pasta Queen, taking turns cranking the handle. Then we'd set the long, cut pieces on the backs of chairs to dry. It looked pretty funny, but tasted incredible.

When we were really little, our grandparents used to let us bring crusty bread to the tables at their restaurant in Pittsburgh. We also baked with our mom. Lots of sweets, cakes, and sometimes breads. We added ingredients, stirred up the mix, and then we would lick the bowl, causing arguments to break out between our parents about how salmonella came from raw eggs that were in the bowl and could now very well be inside us. We almost always ended up laughing, and nobody ever got sick. (It's true though, so don't taste cake mix with raw eggs in it!)

Maybe you've heard about our Web site, Spatulatta.com. A few years ago, Gaylon Emerzian, the producer of the site, was doing a documentary film on the food pyramid and she saw this little boy making pizza. She remembered how excited he was when he told his mom he'd made it all by himself and thought it would be really cool to start a Web site where kids teach kids to cook. When she asked if we'd like to be the hosts, we just couldn't say no.

In 2006, we were the youngest winners ever of a James Beard Foundation Award.* The ceremony in New York was like no other. We were so excited when we arrived and put on our nominee badges and sat in that big auditorium. Our grandmother—Oma—made us good-luck pins. When it was time to announce the winner in our category, Webcasts on Food, Belle and I were rubbing the pins. We were nervous. And then Giada De Laurentiis (star of the Food Network) announced the winner… "Spatulatta-dot-com." We rushed up to the stage to get our medals. Our mom and our Italian grandma, Patti, were both cheering, and our father was speechless.

Cooking is cool because we have fun doing it. We have a great time shooting our videos. Sometimes we make mistakes and they become hilarious outtakes. Then, when we get it just perfect, we brag about whose food is better. Once we've made everything, we get to look at it, taste it, and say, "Wow. I made that all on my own." It's a really good feeling.

We had lots of fun creating this cookbook and we hope you enjoy reading and cooking from it. A couple of last words: Use knives carefully, wash all fruits and veggies before you use them, sometimes adult supervision is necessary (and they'll do the messy parts!), and have fun. If you're having trouble and you just can't seem to get it right, don't get frustrated—it happens to us all the time. Just try it again.

 Liv and Belle

* If you've never heard of James Beard, don't feel bad—we didn't know much about him either until we were nominated for his foundation's award. He was a famous food critic, cookbook author, and cooking teacher, whose friends and colleagues honor him every year by recognizing outstanding chefs and authors and others in the food business with awards for excellence.

## Getting Started

- Wash your hands! Use soap and warm water, and be sure to wash around your nails and between your fingers. Spend enough time under the faucet to sing Old MacDonald or some other rinky-dink song to yourself.

- Make yourself a clean workspace—clear off the kitchen counter or table and wipe down the area. Then get out your recipe and the ingredients and tools you will need. Makes it a heckuva lot easier to cook this way. If you're using them, make sure you wash all fruits and vegetables with cold water.

## Chopping

Lots of recipes are made with chopped onion, so that's what we'll use for our example in this section. When you're just starting out, have an adult help you.

Cut off the top of the onion (the end without the root) and place the flat side of the onion on a cutting board. Cut the onion vertically (straight up and down) in half.

Pull the onion skin back toward the root, but don't take it all the way off. While holding the peeled back skin and part of the onion securely, make five or six cuts down the length

of the onion. Don't slice all the way through though; you want the onion to stay together at its root end.

While carefully curling your fingers back from the blade, start slicing the onion through all the cuts you just made. Make wide slices for a coarse chop, thinner slices for a finer chop. "Mincing" is chopping even finer than finely chopping. Usually you see this term used for garlic cloves.

## Grating & Shredding Cheese

- To shred cheese, use a hand-held cheese grater and a plate or wax paper to catch the cheese. Use the side with the smallest holes for grating hard cheese (like parmesan, our Italian favorite) into finer pieces. To shred soft cheeses, like cheddar or mozzarella, use the side of the grater with larger holes.

- Hold the grater steady with one hand and slide the flat side of the cheese down the grater against the blades. You'll be able to tell if you're doing it right when you see the cheese come out.

- The tricky part is constantly watching your fingers and adjusting where you're holding the cheese so you don't get your fingertips or knuckles near the grater. When the piece of cheese gets too small to grate, Olivia usually eats it, then we get another block of cheese if we still need more for our recipe.

## Separating Eggs

- "Separating" an egg doesn't mean taking it from under a chicken. When you see that in a cookbook, it means the egg white—the runny clear part—has to be separated from the yolk—the bright yellow ball. It's a good idea to have more eggs than you need for your recipe. Belle's friend cracked an egg onto her foot once—good thing we had some extras!

- You'll need two small bowls to separate the egg. Crack the egg by tapping the middle of it on the edge of a small bowl. Too hard—you'll break the yolk. Too soft, you may have lots of little shell pieces to deal with.

- Once the shell has cracked, take two hands and gently separate the shell into two halves over the bowl, holding each piece in one hand. The yolk should be in one of the halves. Gently tip the half without the yoke so that the egg white runs into the bowl.

- Now carefully transfer the yolk to the other shell half. Go slow. Once the yolk seems nearly clear of the white you can drop it into the second bowl. This is

definitely a "practice makes perfect" skill.

- Here's a trick; Olivia can crack the egg, remove the yolk with her hand, then set it down unbroken.

- If there is a little white in with the yolk it is okay. But if there is yolk in with the white you will have to start again because egg whites have to be very clear, especially if you'll be whipping them. Poor egg whites!

## Measuring

- Did you know there's a difference between measuring wet and dry ingredients? Yep, it's true. So here's what you need to measure dry ingredients: plastic or metal cups that come in 1/4, 1/3, 1/2, and 1 cup sizes. You also need measuring spoons that come in sets of 1/4 teaspoon, 1/2 teaspoon, 1 teaspoon, and 1 tablespoon. For liquid measuring, you can use the same spoons, but you'll need different cups that are larger, made of glass or plastic, and have a spout on one end for pouring. These cups are marked on the side with measurements in cup sizes. These measuring cups come in 1 cup, 2 cup, and 4 cup (1 quart) sizes.

- Let's use flour as an example for measuring dry ingredients. Start by loosely spooning the flour into the correct size cup. Don't pack it down.

Then, take the dull, flat side of a knife or your finger and sweep from one side of the cup to the other so the excess flour comes off.

• For liquids, place the measuring cup on a flat surface and pour in the liquid. Bend down so that you are at eye level with the measuring lines. That's important because it's hard to see accurately if you're standing up.

• Measuring liquids using a measuring spoon is easier. Just pour the liquid into the spoon until it fills up but doesn't overflow.

## Setting the Table

• You worked hard on cooking your meal—celebrate your effort by nicely setting the table where you can sit down and enjoy the meal with family or friends. If you've got little brothers or sisters who want to help in the kitchen, this could be a great job for them.

• To set the table for everyday meals, fold napkins and place them to the left with the fork on top. The knife goes on the right side of the plate, with its blade facing the plate. The spoon guards the knife, so it's placed to the right of the knife. As for a bread plate and drinks: Form the thumb and index fingers of both hands into a round "o". You've formed a lower case "b" with your left hand and a "d" with your right. So bread goes on the left, drinks go on the right.

# Cleaning Up & Food Safety

- Food safety is very important to prevent yourself and others from getting sick. Raw eggs, meat, chicken, and fish can contain harmful bacteria that can only be killed by proper cooking and cleaning.

- Always wash your hands and any plates, utensils, or cutting boards with hot, soapy water after handling raw food. Never taste raw meats or eggs.

- It's important to clean up as you go, both for food safety and so there's less work to do when your're finished. Put measuring cups or utensils in the sink when you're done with them, and wash the cutting boards right away or put them in a dishwasher if you have one. Put all ingredients that need to be refrigerated away when you're finished with them so that they don't sit out and scream, "Yo, Bacteria! Over here!"

- After you eat, package up all leftover food and put it in the refrigerator. Don't let your fabulous creations sit out for more than an hour. Most leftovers will keep in the refrigerator for about a week.

- You also have to pay attention to storing uncooked foods properly. Most vegetables last only a few days before they spoil. Raw chicken or meat lasts less—about one or two days. Freezing raw meats after you buy them will allow them to last for as much as six months. If you thaw something that's already been frozen once, don't refreeze it; that causes bacteria to multiply.

## Tooling around in the kitchen

# Cutting boards

We got in big trouble when we used a fork to break apart some cheese on the marble countertop—without using a cutting board. Now we use them all the time. The ones we like the best are made of plastic. If yours slides around on the counter, put a damp dishtowel under it to keep it from moving.

# Food processor

A food processor quickly chops any kind of food into various-sized pieces. The blades for this tool are very sharp, and it's a little tricky learning how to snap the bowl into place. Practice makes perfect on this one, and soon you'll depend on this tool.

# Grater

The easiest one we found has four sides and a handle, so it's pretty stable for a kid. The smaller holes are for scraping fruit skins (for zest), and the bigger holes are for shredding chunks of cheese into small pieces.

# Hand mixer

Belle loves this tool! It makes mixing batter or creaming butter and sugar together a breeze, and makes a good "mad scientist" noise, too. Be careful when you're taking the beaters out of the mixer, though; your fingers can get caught. And never use a spatula or your fingers, when the mixer is turned on.

# Microwave

We consider a microwave oven to be one of the most important tools in our kitchen. It's easy for us to use it and can sometimes be used instead of the cooktop or oven. Remember to wear an oven mitt when you take hot dishes from it. The microwave can be a huge help when thawing frozen food or for speeding up the cooking time.

## Spatula

These guys are "must-haves" in the kitchen. They come in lots of different sizes and materials. Those with flexible edges, especially the rubber kind, help you scrape the sides of bowls when you're mixing and let you get every last bit of mixture out of a bowl and into a pan.

## Tongs

We use this pincher-like metal tool to toss salad and also to take pieces of food from hot pans or pots. It's also useful for moving food around, such as when you're browning meat.

## Potholders/Trivet

Protect your countertops, and your mom will love you! A potholder is made of silicon or fabric. A trivet can be made of metal, or heat-resistant plastic. Place them on tables or counters before you set a hot pot or baking dish on top of it.

## Vegetable peeler

For such a little thing, a swiveled peeler can be hard to handle. It takes the skins off veggies or fruits—something we do pretty often. Scrape off skins in a direction away from you. We've seen TV chefs pull the peeler toward them, but that is too dangerous for us.

## Whisk

This funny-looking wiry thing beats air into a mixture, and makes it light and fluffy. We'll use a whisk when mixing a batter, or beating eggs for omelets, or sometimes whipping cream, for example.

# MEASUREMENT EQUIVALENTS

## Dry/Liquids

1-1/2 teaspoons = 1/2 tablespoon

3 teaspoons = 1 tablespoon

2 tablespoons = 1/8 cup
   (1 fluid ounce)

4 tablespoons =1/4 cup
   (2 fluid ounces)

8 tablespoons = 1/2 cup (4 fluid ounces)

12 tablespoons = 3/4 cup (6 fluid ounces)

16 tablespoons = 1 cup (8 fluid ounces)

1 cup = 1/2 pint (8 fluid ounces)

2 cups = 1 pint (16 fluid ounces)

4 cups = 1 quart

2 pints = 1 quart

4 quarts = 1 gallon

## Butter

1/2 stick butter = 1/4 cup
   (4 tablespoons)

1 stick butter = 1/2 cup
   (8 tablespoons)

2 sticks butter = 1 cup
   (16 tablespoons)

Orange-Carrot Soup

Cloudy with a Chance Meatballs

Green Beans with Garlic

# WINTER

"For this recipe I found out what *puree* and *sauté* mean. Just like vocabulary words at school, I learn some new ones every week. By the way, *puree* means 'to make something smooth' and *sauté* means 'to fry in a small amount of fat.'" —Liv

## You'll Need:

- 2 tablespoons unsalted butter
- 1 cup finely **chopped** onions
- 6 carrots, scrubbed and cut into 1-1/2-inch chunks
- 2 cups chicken stock or canned low-sodium chicken broth
- 1/2 cup freshly squeezed orange juice
- 1/4 cup coarsely chopped, toasted smoked almonds

## Equipment:

- Measuring cups and spoons
- Large heavy-bottomed soup or stockpot (about 8 quarts)
- Ladle
- Food processor or blender
- Individual soup bowls

# Orange-Carrot Soup {Makes enough for 2 adults and 2 children}

1. Melt the butter in the bottom of the stockpot over medium heat. Add the onions and **sauté** until they are translucent (which means they are slightly see-through). If you are old enough to work at the stove, make sure an adult stands by in case you want help.

2. Add the carrots, chicken stock, and orange juice. Turn down the heat and **simmer** until the carrots are tender, about 20 minutes.

3. Turn off the heat and take the pot off the stove.

4. Get a little help ladling the soup from the pot into the food processor. **Puree** the soup, until it is smooth, without lumps.

5. Ladle the hot soup from the processor into the soup bowls. You may need help here, too.

6. Sprinkle the chopped almonds on top of each bowl of soup. Serve this yummy soup immediately.

Sauté onions in butter.

Pour soup into the processor.

Careful when ladling soup into the bowl—hot!

## You'll Need:

- 1 pound boneless, skinless chicken breast halves (2 or 3)
- 1 large red bell pepper, cut in half
- 3 tablespoons extra virgin olive oil
- 1 medium red onion, **chopped**

- 1 to 2 garlic cloves, peeled and finely chopped (about 1 teaspoon)
- 1 pound white mushrooms, wiped clean and cut into 1/4-inch slices
- Salt and freshly ground black pepper to taste
- Chopped fresh parsley for garnish

## Equipment:

- Parchment paper
- Kitchen mallet
- Small heart-shaped cookie cutter
- 12-inch nonstick skillet or frying pan
- Tongs
- Large plate
- Spatula

## Be My Valentine Chicken Sauté

{Makes enough for 2 adults and 2 children}

*Cut heart shapes from red pepper.*

*Heat olive oil in pan.*

1. If you're mad at your sister or brother, this'll help: Put the chicken breasts between two pieces of parchment paper and pound them with the mallet till they're flat, about 1/2 inch thick. Feel better? Good!

2. Have an adult cut the chicken in 1-inch strips. Meanwhile, remove the core and the seeds of the red pepper, and use the cookie cutter to cut out hearts from its flattest parts.

3. Pour the olive oil into the bottom of the skillet and turn on the heat to medium.

4. When the oil is hot, using the tongs, add the chicken strips to the pan and **brown** on both sides. Be patient; it takes about 7 minutes. When one side of the chicken strip is browned, use the tongs to flip it over. Browning seals in the juicy flavor of the chicken.

5. Again, using the tongs, remove the browned chicken from the skillet to the plate and set it aside.

6. Turn the heat up to medium high; add the chopped onion and garlic to the same skillet and **sauté**, stirring frequently with the spatula.

7. When the onion begins to get translucent, add the sliced mushrooms. As the mushrooms begin to soften, return the chicken to the pan so it can warm.

8. Stir in the red pepper hearts and sprinkle with a little salt and pepper.

9. Serve the chicken with the Hearts of Jasmine Rice (page 18), and **garnish** the dish with parsley.

"This is the first dish where I learned how to sauté onions—to cook them until they are almost see-through. This sauté is very yummy, and the little red bell pepper hearts in it will make your heart go pitter-pat." —Belle

"Jasmine rice is from Thailand and actually smells and tastes different from any other rice. Check the back of the package for the cooking time—it might be different from the brand we used." —Liv

Check out other winter recipes at www.spatulatta.com

## You'll Need:

- 1 cup jasmine rice (available in the Asian section of most large grocery stores)
- 1 cup chicken stock or canned low-sodium chicken broth
- 1 cup water
- 1 tablespoon olive oil
- Dash of salt and freshly ground black pepper
- 3 tablespoons **chopped** fresh parsley, plus sprigs for garnish

## Equipment:

- Measuring cups and spoons
- Heavy-bottomed medium saucepan (2 to 3 quarts) with a tight-fitting lid
- Rice paddle or large wooden spoon for stirring
- Small heart-shaped mold (we used cupcake pans)
- Non-flavored cooking spray
- Rubber spatula
- Dinner plates

# Hearts of Jasmine Rice

{Makes 4 servings}

**1.** Add the rice, chicken stock, and water to the saucepan. Add the olive oil, salt, and pepper. Stir.

**2.** Place the saucepan on the stove, cover, and turn on the heat to medium.

**3.** Cook for 20 to 25 minutes or as directed on the package.

**4.** When the rice is ready, remove from the heat. Take off the lid from the pan and let cool until you can handle it safely.

**5.** Meanwhile, prepare the heart-shaped molds. Spray them lightly with nonstick cooking spray and use your fingers to get into all the corners.

**6.** Using the rice paddle or wooden spoon, stir the chopped parsley into the rice.

**7.** Using the spatula, pack the rice into the molds. Press firmly to fill out the heart shape.

**8.** This next step might require some help, depending on how big your hands are. Place a dinner plate top side down over the mold. Holding on to both the plate and the mold, flip them. This is something two people can do together if you count one, two, and flip on the count of three.

**9.** Lift off the mold. The heart-shaped rice should slide out onto the plate. If it doesn't, tap the mold lightly.

**10.** Gently place a serving of chicken **sauté** (see page 16) next to the rice heart and **garnish** with a sprig of parsley.

Chop the parsley.

Stir the rice with a rice paddle.

## You'll Need:

- 2 pounds lean ground beef or ground turkey
- 1 cup fine bread crumbs
- 1 large egg
- 2 garlic cloves, very finely **chopped** (about 1 teaspoon)
- 1 cup very finely chopped onions
- 1 tablespoon dried basil leaves
- 1 teaspoon freshly ground black pepper

## Equipment:

- Measuring cups and spoons
- Cookie sheet (about 16 by 14 inches)
- Aluminum foil
- Large bowl (about 4 quarts)
- Small bowl (such as a cereal bowl)
- Tongs
- Serving bowl

# Cloudy with a Chance Meatballs

{Makes 8 servings}

1. Preheat the oven to 350° F. Cover the cookie sheet with aluminum foil.

2. Put the ground meat into the large bowl; add the bread crumbs.

3. Break the egg into the small bowl, check to make sure you can see no pieces of shell in the bowl, and then pour the egg into the large bowl. Add the garlic, onions, basil, and pepper.

4. This is the fun, slimy part. Use your hands (make sure you wash them first!) to mix and mash all the ingredients together. Make sure the pieces of onion are spread throughout the meat.

5. Take a handful of the meat mixture and roll it to about the size of a Ping-Pong ball. Then place each one on the cookie sheet, about 2 inches apart. Wash those yucky hands thoroughly!

6. **Bake** until the meatballs are **browned** on all sides, 11 or 12 minutes.

7. When they are cooked, use the tongs to put the meatballs into the serving bowl.

8. You can serve them with hot pasta and your favorite spaghetti sauce, or eat them just as they are—delicious!

Put ingredients into large bowl.

Get messy! Roll into balls.

Place 2 inches apart on cookie sheet.

"I think everybody will love this.
It's one of those recipes where you get to be
real messy and mix the ingredients with your hands.
I eat these meatballs with waves of spaghetti, just
like they do in the town of Chewandswallow. After
dinner, read—or ask your mom or dad to read the
book to you—Cloudy with a Chance of
Meatballs by Judi Barrett."—Liv

"This is a fun, fast gift to make for anyone who loves chocolate. My grandmother gave me this recipe, and I'm telling you—it works!" —Belle

## You'll Need:

- 3 cups (large 12-ounce package plus small 6-ounce package) semisweet or milk chocolate chips
- 4 tablespoons (1/2 stick) unsalted butter
- 1 can (14 ounces) sweetened condensed milk

## Equipment:

- Measuring cups and spoons
- Double boiler or a metal bowl set inside a saucepan
- Large metal or wooden spoon for stirring
- 8 by 8-inch glass baking dish
- Plastic wrap
- Cutting board (at least 8 inches across)
- Pizza cutter

 # Extra E-Z Fudge

{Makes 24 1-inch squares}

1. Fill the bottom of the double boiler or the saucepan halfway with water and set it on the stove.

2. Place the chocolate chips, butter, and condensed milk in the top half of the double boiler or in the metal bowl and stir with the spoon. The mixture will be sticky—do your best. Turn on the heat to medium low.

3. Slowly melt the chips, butter, and condensed milk together, stirring every few minutes. It will take about 10 minutes.

4. Meanwhile, line the glass baking dish with plastic wrap, enough so that the wrap flops over the edges of the pan on all sides.

5. When the chocolate chips have all melted and the mixture is smooth, remove the top pan of the double boiler or the bowl from the heat and pour the mixture into the prepared dish.

6. To get that wonderful creamy texture, let the fudge cool completely. You can hurry the process by putting the baking dish in a larger pan filled with cold water. After the fudge cools, put the dish in the fridge for at least an hour.

7. To unmold: It works really well if two people grab the ends of the plastic wrap and lift up, pulling the block of fudge out of the dish. Transfer the fudge to the cutting board or other flat surface.

8. Use the pizza cutter to cut the fudge into 1-inch squares. Now it's ready to serve or pack up in a pretty tin and give as a gift.

Slowly melt ingredients in the top of a double boiler.

Pour into a dish lined with plastic wrap.

A pizza cutter makes a great tool to cut fudge into pieces.

# POMEGRANATE AND PINK GRAPEFRUIT SALAD

## You'll Need:

- 3 tablespoons honey
- 2 tablespoons rice wine vinegar
- 1 large pink grapefruit
- 1-1/2 cups green or red seedless grapes, cut in half
- 1 cup broken walnut pieces
- 1 pomegranate

## Equipment:

- Measuring cups and spoons
- Small bowl or teacup for the dressing
- Large bowl (about 4 quarts)
- Large metal or wooden spoon for stirring
- Plastic wrap

# Pomegranate and Pink Grapefruit Salad

{Makes 4 servings}

1. Mix the honey and rice vinegar in the small bowl until well combined; set aside. This is the salad dressing.

2. Peel the pinkish yellow rind and the pith (the stringy white inner skin) of the grapefruit. Have an adult cut the fruit into 1-inch pieces (you should have about 2 cups). Place the grapefruit in the large bowl.

3. Add the grape halves and walnut pieces and stir the mixture with the spoon.

4. Here comes the tricky part because the bright red juice of the pomegranate can really stain. You'll need an adult's help. When you cut off the top and bottom of the fruit, you'll see how the seeds are arranged in sections. Make shallow slices through the red skin between the sections. Slip your finger in between one section and the center. If you pull very gently, you can free an entire section of bright red seeds. Separate the seeds from the yellow bases and sprinkle them into the large bowl.

5. Drizzle the honey dressing over the fruit and mix thoroughly, but gently, so you don't break the pomegranate seeds.

6. Cover the salad with plastic wrap and put it in the refrigerator for at least 1 hour to let the flavors blend. The salad is best when it sits in the fridge overnight. Stir the salad again before serving.

Peel the grapefruit.

Pull seeds from the pomegranate.

Taa-daa! You're going to love this salad.

"Pomegranates are an 'exotic' fruit that have a flower end that sticks out and a stem end that looks a lot like a belly button. To peel one, you pull off the red skin and the yellow stuff underneath it. Then you'll see the really bright red seeds. They're like buried treasure!" —Liv

"You can make these cookies using any big and little cookie cutters you like. We used the Amish heart-in-hand. For my birthday one year, we made leaf-shaped cookies with a smaller leaf shape filled with orange candies. Mom calls them stained-glass cookies—the kids loved holding them up to see the light shine through the candy cutout." —Belle

Carefully measure dry ingredients.

Roll dough to 1/8 inch thick.

Pour candy chunks into the cutout.

## You'll Need:

- 12 tablespoons (1-1/2 sticks) salted butter, softened
- 1 cup sugar
- 2 large eggs
- 1 teaspoon pure vanilla extract
- 2-1/2 cups all-purpose flour, plus a little extra for rolling and cutting the dough
- 1 teaspoon baking powder
- 1 teaspoon salt
- 12 to 15 clear red hard candies (we used red Life Savers)

## Equipment:

- Measuring cups and spoons
- Large mixing bowl
- Hand mixer
- Plastic wrap
- Rolling pin
- Heart-in-hand cookie cutter set or a large heart-shaped cookie cutter and a smaller heart-shaped cookie cutter that will fit inside it
- 2 to 3 cookie sheets (about 16 by 14 inches each)
- Small resealable plastic storage bag
- Kitchen mallet

 # Heart-in-Hand Cookies {Makes 30 cookies}

1. Put the butter and sugar in a bowl and **beat** them together until they are a light lemon color and very smooth.

2. Add the eggs and vanilla, then beat again until smooth.

3. Now add the 2-1/2 cups flour, the baking powder, and salt. Mix together.

4. Using your hands, form one or two balls of cookie dough, wrap each in plastic, and chill them for about an hour.

5. Preheat the oven to 375° F.

6. Sprinkle the counter and your rolling pin with flour and roll out the dough until it is 1/8 inch thick.

7. Cut out your larger shape and transfer it to the cookie sheet.

8. When the larger cookie is safely on the sheet, cut out the smaller shape.

9. To prevent a giant mess, put the candy in a baggie and crush it with a rolling pin or mallet.

10. Cut a hole in one corner of the plastic bag and pour the red candy chunks in the smaller cutout, almost filling the hole.

11. **Bake** at 375° F for 7 to 9 minutes, or until the cookies are slightly brown.

12. Take them out of the oven and cool them on the cookie sheet. Be patient! The cookies and their candy centers must be completely cool before you try to lift them off the sheet or else the heart will be left behind. Pretty neat, huh?

# GREEN BEANS WITH GARLIC

## You'll Need:

- 1 pound green beans, washed and trimmed
- 1/4 cup water
- 1 to 2 garlic cloves, peeled
- 3 tablespoons unsalted butter or extra virgin olive oil

## Equipment:

- Measuring cups and spoons
- Kitchen shears or scissors
- Large glass or microwave-safe bowl
- Plastic wrap
- Microwave oven
- Mini food processor, optional
- 10-inch skillet or frying pan
- Large metal or wooden spoon for stirring

## Green Beans with Garlic {Makes 4 to 6 servings}

**1.** Place the beans in the microwave-safe bowl. Add the water, cover with plastic wrap, and **microwave** on high until just tender, about 5 minutes.

**2.** While the beans are cooking, mince the garlic. That means to cut it up into really teeny pieces. (You can have an adult help with a mini food processor, if you like.)

**3.** Melt the butter or oil in the skillet over medium heat. Add the garlic and **sauté** until you smell that great garlic aroma, about 2 to 3 minutes.

**4.** When the beans are ready, remove them from the microwave—be careful of the steam; it will be very hot—and put them in the skillet. This is a good time to ask an adult for help.

**5.** Stir the beans gently until they are coated with the garlic butter or oil. Mmmmmm!

Trim the ends from the beans.

Mince the garlic—this is the easy way.

Delish!

"A kebab is usually some kind of meat roasted on a stick. Our friend Nicky is Armenian, and he told me this is the winter version of kebabs. You make it when you're too cold to stand outside to roast the meat." —Belle

## You'll Need:

- 2 tablespoons unsalted butter or extra virgin olive oil
- 1 pound lean lamb cut from the leg into chunks, or use beef stew meat
- 2 medium onions, **chopped**
- 1 teaspoon salt
- 1/2 teaspoon freshly ground black pepper
- 1/2 teaspoon sweet paprika
- 2 red or orange sweet bell peppers, cut into 1-inch wide strips
- 1 cup water
- 4 to 6 tablespoons tomato paste
- 1 tablespoon tarragon vinegar

## Equipment:

- Measuring cups and spoons
- Heavy-bottomed Dutch oven (6 to 8 quarts) with a tight-fitting lid
- Plate
- Large metal or wooden spoon for stirring
- Small bowl
- Ladle
- Serving bowl or individual plates

# Tass Kebab {Makes 4 to 6 servings}

1. Melt the butter or heat the oil in the Dutch oven over medium heat.

2. Add the meat, letting it **brown** on one side, then turn it over to let the other side brown. Remove the meat from the pot and place on the plate; set aside.

3. Using the same pot, add the onions and **sauté** until translucent (see-through).

4. When the onions are ready, spoon the meat back into the pot and stir in the salt, pepper, and paprika. Add the bell pepper strips.

5. In the small bowl, combine the water and tomato paste and stir until well mixed. Pour the mixture into the pot. If it isn't enough to cover all the meat and vegetables, add some more water until it does. Cover the pot and cook over low heat until the meat is tender, about 45 minutes.

6. About 15 minutes before the stew is done, stir in the vinegar.

7. Ladle the stew into the serving bowl or onto individual plates. Serve immediately with rice.

*Brown the meat in a pot.*

*Add meat back into your sauté.*

*Combine water and tomato paste.*

# STONE SOUP

## You'll Need:

- 4 dried black mushrooms, soaked in warm water for at least 1 hour and drained
- 4 cups chicken stock or canned low-sodium chicken broth, heated
- 3 "stones" (small whole potatoes, scrubbed with their skins; see Note)
- 1 large onion, thinly sliced
- 1 large carrot, scrubbed and cut into 1/4-inch rounds
- 3 garlic cloves, peeled and minced
- 1-inch piece ginger, peeled and shredded (1 tablespoon)
- 4 ounces lean chicken or pork, cut into 1/4-inch strips

- 1/2 cup snow peas, washed and strings removed, if necessary
- 1 cup shredded Chinese cabbage
- 1 small can (5 ounces) bamboo shoots, drained
- 1 slab (10 ounces) firm bean curd (also called tofu), cut into cubes
- 3 tablespoons soy sauce, preferably low sodium
- 2 teaspoons sesame oil
- 2 tablespoons cornstarch
- 3 tablespoons cold water
- 1 large egg, beaten
- 1/2 teaspoon white pepper, optional
- 2 tablespoons rice wine vinegar, optional
- 1 scallion, thinly sliced

## Equipment:

- Measuring spoons and cups
- Medium saucepan (2 to 3 quarts)
- Large heavy-bottomed soup or stockpot (about 8 quarts)
- Large metal or wooden spoon for stirring
- Teacup or small bowl
- Individual soup bowls

## Stone Soup {Makes 12 to 16 servings}

1. Slice the black mushrooms into 1/4-inch strips.

2. Just before you are ready to start the soup, bring the chicken stock or broth to a boil in the saucepan.

3. Put the potatoes in the bottom of the stockpot.

4. Now invite your friends to add the onion, carrot, garlic, ginger, black mushrooms, meat, and the heated chicken stock.

Cut chicken into strips.

Add veggies and garlic.

Serve the soup hot!

"Stone soup requires lots of teamwork, just like in the story. We invited all the neighbor kids over, read the story by Jon J. Muth, the Chinese version of the Stone Soup legend, and then they each put something in the pot." —Liv

**5.** Turn on the heat to medium high and bring the soup to a boil. When the meat has turned from pink to beige, lower the heat to a **simmer** (that is, lower the heat slightly).

**6.** Now, add the snow peas, shredded cabbage, bamboo shoots, and bean curd. Simmer for about 7 minutes.

**7.** Add the soy sauce and sesame oil. Stir gently so you don't break up the bean curd.

**8.** In the teacup or small bowl, mix the cornstarch and water until smooth. Gently drizzle the mixture into the soup. You can ask an adult to stir while you pour in the mixture a little at a time.

**9.** Slowly drizzle the **beaten** egg into the soup. The hot soup will cook the egg as it falls into the water, so pour just a little swirl of egg at a time.

**10.** If you would like hot-and-sour soup—the kind you get at a Chinese restaurant—make the soup spicy by adding the optional white pepper and rice wine vinegar. Stir in the sliced scallion.

**11.** Serve the soup immediately in individual soup bowls.

**NOTE:** Please don't use real stones: They might contain some minerals you really don't want to eat! You can find dried black mushrooms, sesame oil, and Chinese cabbage in the Asian section of most grocery stores and at Asian markets.

# RECIPE NOTES

..........................................................................................................................

..........................................................................................................................

..........................................................................................................................

..........................................................................................................................

..........................................................................................................................

..........................................................................................................................

..........................................................................................................................

..........................................................................................................................

..........................................................................................................................

..........................................................................................................................

..........................................................................................................................

..........................................................................................................................

..........................................................................................................................

..........................................................................................................................

..........................................................................................................................

..........................................................................................................................

..........................................................................................................................

SPRING

Spectacular Spring Recipes!

Curly Creole
Salad

A Spring
Basket

Irish Soda
Bread

# SPRING

# BUNNY SALAD

"Mom used to have this when she was a kid. We like it because you can create a little scene with your bunny, like he's eating strawberries in a patch. Sometimes, I'm sad to eat him!" —Belle

## You'll Need:

- 8 large romaine lettuce leaves
- 4 large (about 2-1/2 inches long) slices of carrot, about 1/4-inch thick, cut on the diagonal, so they form oval shapes
- 2 ripe fresh pears, preferably Bosc or Bartlett
- 12 whole cloves
- 1/4 cup cottage cheese
- 12 whole strawberries, rinsed and drained on paper towels

## Equipment:

- Measuring cups and spoons
- Paper towels
- 4 small plates
- Kitchen scissors or shears
- Swivel peeler

 # Bunny Salad {Makes 4 bunny salads}

**1.** Rinse the lettuce leaves and pat them dry between two pieces of paper towel. Lay them out on the plates. This is the grass for your bunnies to rest on.

**2.** Cut the carrot pieces in half the long way with the scissors or shears. Lay out the halves in matching pairs. These will be your bunny ears.

**3.** Peel the pears with the peeler. Cut the pears in half the long way. (Ask for help if you need it.) Remove the seeds and place the pears cut side down on top of the lettuce leaves.

**4.** In the small end of the pear, push in 2 cloves about 3/4 inch from the end, for the eyes; push 1 clove in at the very end, for the nose.

**5.** Cut a slit about 1/2 inch behind the eyes. Push 2 carrot ears into the slit.

**6.** Place 1 tablespoon cottage cheese next to the round end of each pear. There's the bunny's cottontail.

**7.** Arrange a few strawberries on the lettuce around the bunny. Now it looks as if the bunny has hopped into the strawberry patch!

Insert the carrot "ears" into the slit in the pear.

Add cottage cheese tail.

Bunny in the berry patch!

Peel the bananas.

## You'll Need:

- 3 large bananas
- 1 large semisweet chocolate bar (3-1/2 to 4 ounces) or 1 small bag semisweet chocolate chips (6 ounces)

## Equipment:

- 6 craft sticks or skinny wooden forks
- Large resealable plastic freezer storage bag
- Small microwavable bowl (1 to 1-1/2 quarts); we found that an oval one works best
- Microwave oven
- Large wooden spoon for stirring
- Large sheet of wax paper
- Cookie sheet

Carefully insert sticks into banana halves.

# Go Bananas!

{Makes 6 chocolate bananas}

1. Peel the bananas and slice them in half.

2. Push 1 craft stick or fork into the cut end of each banana half. (Insert as far as necessary to keep the banana stable, but not so far that you can't use the stick as a handle.)

3. When you have all your bananas on sticks, carefully place them in the plastic bag, seal, and freeze them for at least 2 hours.

4. When the bananas are frozen, make the chocolate coating. Break the bar of chocolate into pieces and place in the microwavable bowl or empty the bag of chocolate chips into the bowl.

5. **Microwave** on high for about 30 seconds. (Watch closely because chocolate can hold its shape as it melts.) Remove from the microwave and stir with the wooden spoon. If it's not all the way melted, continue to heat the chocolate 10 seconds at a time, being careful that it doesn't burn.

6. Lay out the sheet of wax paper on a cookie sheet.

7. Roll each frozen banana in the melted chocolate or pour it over the bananas with a spoon. (The coldness of the banana will make the chocolate harden into a shell.) As each banana is coated in chocolate, place it on the wax paper.

8. When all the bananas are coated, and their shells have hardened, wrap the wax paper around them and slide the cookie sheet into the freezer for another hour. When they're completely frozen, you can take them off the cookie sheet and put them in a sealed freezer bag where they'll keep for up to two weeks.

Melt chocolate in a microwave.

"This is one of my favorites. It does take a little while, so I like to do the first part of the recipe before school. Then when I get home, I do the chocolate part and then my favorite—the eating part!"—Liv

"It's fun to learn about all the different kinds of greens that can be made into a salad. This recipe uses curly endive, Belgian endive, and romaine lettuce. With the dressing, it's perfect." —Liv

Check out other salad recipes at www.spatulatta.com

## You'll Need:
- 1 head Belgian endive, pulled apart into leaves
- 1 head curly endive, pulled apart into leaves
- 1 small head romaine lettuce, pulled apart into leaves
- 2 medium ripe red tomatoes
- 1 red bell pepper

### For Old-fashioned French Dressing
- 1 small can (6 ounces) tomato paste
- 1 cup salad oil, such as extra virgin olive oil or canola oil
- 3/4 cup apple cider vinegar
- 3 tablespoons sugar
- 1 teaspoon salt

## Equipment:
- Salad spinner or paper towels for drying
- 6 individual salad plates
- Soup spoon

### For Old-fashioned French Dressing
- Measuring cups and spoons
- Blender
- Wide-mouth jar for storing

*Separate leaves of Belgian endive.*

 # Curly Creole Salad
{Makes 6 Creole salads}

1. Rinse both types of endive and the romaine. Dry the leaves in the salad spinner or between the paper towels.

2. Tear the romaine into 1-inch pieces and arrange them on each of the plates.

3. Arrange the Belgian endive leaves like spokes on the plates.

4. Break off curly portions of the curly endive and arrange them around the edges of the plate.

5. Cut the tomatoes into 1/2-inch cubes and the red pepper into 3/4-inch chunks.

6. Spoon a pile of tomatoes and red pepper chunks on top of the greens on each salad plate.

 # Old-fashioned French Dressing
{Makes 2 cups dressing}

1. Put all the ingredients together in the blender and blend well.

2. Taste the dressing. You might like to add a little more sugar or a little more salt.

3. Drizzle on your Curly Creole Salad, or pour into the wide-mouth jar, cover, and refrigerate. Leftover dressing will keep for up to 2 weeks.

*Top the greens with tomatoes and peppers.*

## You'll Need:

- 1 recipe Microwave Roux
- 1 large onion, coarsely **chopped**
- 1 large green bell pepper, coarsely chopped
- 3 celery ribs, coarsely chopped
- 4 garlic cloves, peeled and finely chopped
- 1/2 teaspoon freshly ground black pepper, optional
- 1/4 teaspoon ground cayenne (red pepper), optional
- 3 cups chicken stock or canned low-sodium chicken broth

- 1 package (1 pound) smoked turkey sausage, sliced diagonally, about 1/2-inch thick
- 2 cups cubed cooked chicken
- 1/2 cup finely chopped fresh parsley
- 3 whole scallions, sliced in 1/2-inch rounds
- 1 pound okra, stems trimmed off, cut in 1-inch chunks
- Cooked brown or white rice, optional, for serving

### For Microwave Roux
- 2/3 cup vegetable oil, such as canola oil
- 2/3 cup all-purpose flour

## Equipment:

- Measuring cups and spoons
- Large heavy-bottomed soup pot or stockpot (about 8 quarts) with a tight-fitting lid
- Large metal or wooden spoon for stirring
- 6 individual soup bowls

### For Microwave Roux
- 4- or 8-cup heatproof glass measuring cup
- Fork or whisk
- Oven mitts or pot holders

Sauté the onion, peppers and celery.

Add okra to the gumbo.

# Yumbo Gumbo

{Makes 6 good-size servings}

1. Scoop the roux into the soup pot or stockpot. Add the onion, green pepper, and celery and mix with the spoon until all the vegetables are covered with roux.

2. Turn on the heat to medium and **sauté** the vegetables until the onion is soft and translucent (see-through).

3. Add the garlic, and the black pepper and cayenne, if using. Stir.

4. Add the chicken stock, sausage, chicken, parsley, and scallions. Stir.

5. Cover the pot, turn the heat to low, and cook for 1 hour, stirring occasionally.

6. Uncover the pot and stir in the okra.

7. Put the lid back on the pot and cook on low for another 30 minutes, stirring occasionally so the gumbo doesn't stick to the bottom of the pot.

8. Serve the gumbo in soup bowls, accompanied by rice, if desired.

"I'd never tasted okra before I made this dish. Miss Gaylon, our producer, says it's traditional to cut off little pieces of okra and stick them to your face. We tried it and it works! I don't know if that's supposed to make better gumbo, but this recipe is awesome." —Belle

#  Microwave Roux {Makes 2 cups of roux}

1. Place the oil and flour in the measuring cup. Mix until well blended.

2. Put the uncovered measuring cup in the **microwave**. Cook on high for 6 minutes.

3. Carefully remove the measuring cup from the microwave. Oil gets much hotter than water. The roux will be a very light brown, and the surface will be bumpy. The color you want it to be is peanut-buttered-colored.

4. **Whisk** out the lumps and return it to the microwave for another 2 minutes. The roux will start to give off a nutty aroma.

5. Each microwave is different, so check the roux to determine if you need to cook it for another minute or two.

6. When the roux has reached the desired color, remove it from the microwave and stir one last time.

7. Let the roux stand and cool. You can pour off a little of the excess oil, but don't pour off all of it because you will need some oil to **sauté** your vegetables correctly. Be safe! Have fun!

## You'll Need:

- 6- to 8-inch Easter basket
- 2 clear plastic bags (such as those you put veggies in at the grocery store)
- 2 to 3 quarts potting soil (about 3 times as much soil as perlite)
- Perlite
- 2 cups wheat berries, presoaked overnight
- Water
- Colored eggs or treats, optional (see Note)

## Equipment:

- Large metal or wooden spoon or scoop
- Large bowl (about 4 quarts)
- Kitchen scissors or shears

# It's Alive! A Spring Basket

### {Makes 1 beautiful basket}

1. Line the inside of your basket with one of the plastic bags. Make sure it doesn't have holes because you'll be putting soil and water in the basket.

2. Mix the potting soil and perlite together in the large bowl with a spoon. Fill the basket with the soil mixture.

3. Spread a thick layer of wheat berries on top of the soil. Gently press them into the soil.

4. Pour about a cup of water slowly over the berries, making sure every area gets wet.

5. Cover your whole basket with the second bag. You may have to cut a slit in it to fit it over your basket. The bag doesn't have to be tight, it just needs to keep the moisture in.

6. Place the basket in a sunny window. Every day, remove the plastic bag and spritz the wheat berries with water to keep them moist. Recover the basket.

7. In 5 or 6 days, you'll have a very hairy basket! For that beautiful groomed-lawn look, use your scissors or shears to cut the wheat grass to about 1 inch above the basket's edge.

8. If you like, put your colored eggs or treats in the basket and enjoy the compliments!

NOTE: If you leave the colored eggs out as a decoration, you can't eat them.

Spread wheat berries over the soil.

It'll sprout in just days!

A good haircut makes a great basket.

"Yes, it's real grass! These baskets make a great centerpiece or a supercool gift for someone special. Start the basket about a week before you need it. Keep it inside so the nosy little (real) bunnies can't eat it. Ha, ha, ha." —Belle

Add ingredients to a microwave-safe bowl.

Cut out star shapes from bread.

Toast!

## You'll Need:

- 4 large eggs
- 2 tablespoons salted butter
- 4 tablespoons water
- 1/2 cup shredded Swiss cheese
- 1/2 cup **diced** smoked turkey breast
- 1/2 cup defrosted and well-drained frozen spinach
- 2 or 4 slices white bread
- 2 or 4 slices whole wheat bread

## Equipment:

- Measuring cups and spoons
- Large microwavable bowl (about 4 quarts)
- Nonstick olive oil cooking spray
- Large metal or wooden spoon for stirring
- Microwave oven
- Oven mitts
- Small star-shaped cookie cutter
- 1 or 2 serving plates

 # Microwave Scramblette with Star Toast

{Makes enough for 1 adult and 1 child}

**1.** Coat the inside of the microwavable bowl with the cooking spray.

**2.** Break the eggs into the bowl. Add the butter, water, cheese, turkey, and spinach and stir well with the spoon.

**3.** Place the bowl in the **microwave** and cook on high for about 4 minutes. Check after 2 minutes or so to see how fast your microwave is cooking the eggs.

**4.** Take the bowl out of the microwave. The eggs will be cooked around the sides but the middle will still be liquid. Scrape the cooked eggs off the sides of the bowl and stir into the liquid eggs. Cook on high for another minute or so.

**5.** Check your eggs again. If they still need to cook some more, repeat step 4. When they're done, the eggs will look like traditionally scrambled eggs. (Our microwave took 6 minutes total to cook the eggs.) Use the oven mitts to take the eggs out of the microwave.

**6.** Place 1 slice of white and 1 slice of whole wheat bread on a counter and cut a star shape from the middle of each slice. Put the white star into the cutout space of the wheat bread and the wheat star into the white bread.

**7.** Toast the bread. Repeat for 2 servings. Place 2 slices of toast on each plate. When the eggs are cooked, place a serving next to the toast. Pretty neat, huh?

## You'll Need:

- 3 pounds red potatoes, peeled and cut into 1-inch chunks
- 6 tablespoons salted butter
- 1/4 cup whole or 2% milk
- 3 tablespoons vegetable oil, such as canola
- 1 medium onion, **chopped** (about 3/4 cup)
- 2-1/2 pounds ground lamb
- 1 tablespoon all-purpose flour
- 1 cup chicken stock or canned low-sodium chicken broth
- 1 tablespoon fresh thyme leaves or 1 teaspoon dried
- 1 tablespoon fresh rosemary leaves or 1 teaspoon dried
- Pinch of ground nutmeg
- Salt and freshly ground black pepper to taste
- 1 cup frozen peas
- 1 cup **diced** cooked carrots
- 1/4 cup (1/2 stick) salted butter, melted
- 1/4 cup freshly grated Parmesan cheese

## Equipment:

- Measuring cups and spoons
- Large saucepan (4 to 6 quarts)
- Long-handled fork
- Large colander or sieve
- Large bowl (about 4 quarts)
- Potato masher
- 14-inch skillet or frying pan
- Metal spatula
- Large metal or wooden spoon for stirring
- Large rectangular casserole dish (about 6 quarts)
- Rubber spatula
- Pastry brush

# Shepherd's Pie
{Makes 8 to 10 hearty servings}

**1.** Put the cut potatoes into the saucepan and add enough water to cover them (about 2 quarts). Turn on the heat and bring to a **boil**.

**2.** Cook the potatoes until the tines of the fork slide easily in and out of the potato chunks.

**3.** Turn off the heat. The pot will be very hot and heavy, so have an adult drain the potatoes into the colander or sieve.

Put some muscle into mashing the spuds.

Brown your meat.

This dish has the "no leftover" guarantee!

"Our friend Maggie in Pittsburgh makes this when her big Irish family is coming over for dinner. We're lucky because she shared her grandmother's recipe with us." —Liv

4. Transfer the potatoes to the large bowl. Add the 6 tablespoons butter and the milk and mash it all together with the potato masher. Leave some chunks for a chewy texture. Set aside.

5. Preheat the oven to 350° F.

6. Heat the oil in the skillet. Add the onion and **sauté** over medium-high heat until translucent (see-through), about 3 minutes.

7. Add the lamb to the skillet and cook, turning it gently with the metal spatula every few minutes until it is **browned** on all sides, about 5 to 6 minutes.

8. Pour off the fat. We used a large sieve to make sure we didn't lose any of the meat (see Note).

9. Return the meat to the skillet. Sprinkle the flour over the meat and use the large spoon to stir until well mixed.

10. Pour in the chicken stock or broth. Add the thyme, rosemary, nutmeg, salt, and pepper. Cook until thickened, about 15 minutes. Stir in the peas and carrots.

11. Let the mixture cool for a few minutes, then spoon it into the bottom of the casserole dish.

12. Top the meat mixture with dollops of the mashed potatoes. Use the rubber spatula to spread the potatoes around in a motion kind of like frosting a cake. Try not to mix the meat in with the potatoes as you spread the top layer.

13. Brush the melted butter evenly over the potatoes and sprinkle on the Parmesan cheese.

14. Place the casserole dish in the oven and cook until warmed through and the top is golden brown, about 35 minutes.

NOTE: To drain the fat from the meat, put a bowl in the sink, and line it with a single piece of aluminum foil. Place the sieve in the bowl and have an adult pour the meat in. After you transfer the meat back to the skillet, place the bowl in the refrigerator until the fat sets. Fold up the sides of the foil and throw it in the garbage.

# IRISH SODA BREAD

## You'll Need:

- 5 cups all-purpose flour
- 1 teaspoon salt
- 1 teaspoon baking soda
- 5 teaspoons baking powder
- 1/2 cup (1 stick) unsalted butter, softened
- 2 large eggs, **beaten** slightly

- 1-1/4 cups black raisins
- 3/4 cup sugar
- 1-1/2 to 2 cups regular or low-fat cultured buttermilk

## Equipment:

- Measuring cups and spoons
- Large metal or wooden spoon for stirring
- Large bowl (about 4 quarts)
- Cookie sheet (about 16 by 14 inches)
- Butter knife

Add butter and stir til crumbly.

Flour your hands and the counter for smooth sailing.

 ## Irish Soda Bread

{Makes 2 loaves of soda bread}

1. Preheat the oven to 375° F.

2. Stir together the flour, salt, soda, and baking powder in the bowl.

3. Unwrap the butter and set aside the wrapper, which you'll use to **grease** the cookie sheet. Stir the butter into the flour mixture until it is crumbly.

4. Add the eggs, raisins, and sugar. Stir well, then use your clean hands and fists to scoop the dry ingredients from the bottom of the bowl and gently push them into the dough.

5. With an adult, add the buttermilk, a little at a time, until the dough is sticky. One person stirs while the other slowly pours the buttermilk.

6. Sprinkle flour on the counter or flat surface, remove the dough and shape into rounds.

7. **Knead** the dough ten times. **Fold** and press, then turn the dough. Repeat ten times. Kneading gives the bread its good texture.

8. Cut the dough in half and shape it into 2 rounds.

9. Rub the cookie sheet all over with the buttered side of the wrapper.

10. When your loaves are on the sheet, use a floured butter knife to cut into, but not all the way through, the tops of the bread, in an "X" shape. This is called **scoring**.

11. **Bake** the bread for 45 to 60 minutes until the bread is a nice nutty brown.

"This bread uses baking soda instead of yeast to make it rise. It has a sweet taste and looks great right out of the oven. I like it because we don't have to wait for the dough to rise and rise again like we would if we used yeast." —Liv

# RECIPE NOTES

..........................................................................................................
..........................................................................................................
..........................................................................................................
..........................................................................................................
..........................................................................................................
..........................................................................................................
..........................................................................................................
..........................................................................................................
..........................................................................................................
..........................................................................................................
..........................................................................................................
..........................................................................................................
..........................................................................................................
..........................................................................................................
..........................................................................................................
..........................................................................................................

SUMMER

Sizzlin' Summer Recipes!

Kalbi Beef

Wiener
Weenie Dogs

Sweet Potato
Pie

# SUMMER

"This yummy pesto is one of those recipes you really can't mess up. But Papa says the secret is using the kind of Parmesan cheese that comes in a big wedge or chunk—not the kind you shake out of a jar, plastic container, or cardboard tube." —Belle

## You'll Need:

- 2 ounces good-quality Parmesan cheese, cut into chunks (about 1/2 cup)
- 2 cups washed, dried, and firmly packed fresh basil leaves
- 1/2 cup extra virgin olive oil
- 1/4 cup pine nuts or coarsely **chopped** walnuts
- 6 garlic cloves, peeled

## Equipment:

- Measuring cups and spoons
- Food processor
- Rubber spatula

 # Papa's Pesto {Makes enough to toss with 1 pound of cooked pasta}

**1.** Put the Parmesan cheese in the bowl of the food processor, lock the lid, and process until the cheese is finely **chopped** and resembles grains of rice. Add the basil and process until it is also finely chopped. (You might have to use the spatula to scrape down the sides of the food processor bowl after this step.)

**2.** Here's the cool part. Put the lid back on and, with the food processor running, pour the olive oil through the feed tube on top. Mix until the oil combines with the basil and cheese. (Scrape down the sides of the bowl if the mixture is not well combined.)

**3.** Add the pine nuts and process only as long as it takes to count to 3 slowly. Add the garlic and process again until the mixture is creamy. (Scrape down the sides again if needed.)

**4.** Pesto is often used as a sauce for meat, or as a topping for bruschetta. I like to use it instead of mayonnaise on a sandwich!

*Use fresh ingredients.*          *Add basil and cheese to processor.*          *Add the olive oil.*

*Arrange tomato slices.*

*Place the soft mozzarella slices on top.*

*A grind of fresh pepper tops it all off.*

## You'll Need:

- 3 big ripe red tomatoes
- 4 balls fresh buffalo mozzarella cheese (about 1 pound total)
- 12 fresh basil leaves (pretty big ones)
- Extra virgin olive oil
- Salt and freshly ground black pepper to taste

## Equipment:

- Butter knife
- Pretty serving plate (round is good if you want to arrange the tomatoes and cheese in overlapping rings)

# Caprese Salad {Makes 6 salads}

1. Have an adult cut the tomatoes into 1/2-inch slices.

2. Meanwhile, use a butter knife to cut the cheese into slices about as thick as the tomatoes'.

3. Arrange the tomato and cheese slices on the plate, overlapping them to make rings, or make another pretty design. Place the basil leaves on top of the slices of tomatoes and cheese.

4. Drizzle a skinny stream of olive oil over the salad in a zigzag motion. Sprinkle a little salt and a few grinds of pepper over the salad, and your Italian flag is ready to eat!

"Did you know that this salad looks like an Italian flag? Seriously, the Caprese Salad comes from Italy, and its red tomatoes, green basil, and white mozzarella cheese are the three colors of that country's flag. Grandma serves a lot of these at her restaurant." —Belle

# BLUEBERRY PIE

"This delicious pie is from our friend Karen Duffin. Make sure you pinch the edges of the piecrusts together really tightly or the filling could drip out of your pie plate and burn on the bottom of the oven. This happened to us, and we thought the pie had exploded—lots of smoke—but it tasted really good anyway." —Liv

## You'll Need:

- 5 cups fresh blueberries
- 1 tablespoon freshly squeezed lemon juice
- 1/2 cup sugar
- 1 tablespoon unsalted butter
- 2 tablespoons cornstarch
- 2 prepared piecrusts (like the kind that come rolled up in a 15-ounce box)

## Equipment:

- Measuring cups and spoons
- Colander
- Medium saucepan (2 to 3 quarts)
- Large metal or wooden spoon for stirring
- 9-inch pie plate
- Butter knife
- Cooling rack

 # Blueberry Pie {Makes 6 to 8 servings}

1. Preheat the oven to 400° F.

2. Rinse the berries under cold water and let them drain in a colander in the sink.

3. Put 4 cups of the blueberries in the saucepan (save 1 cup for later). Add the lemon juice, sugar, butter, and cornstarch to the saucepan and place it on the stove. Turn on the heat to medium. You want the mixture to start **boiling**, so when it gets bubbly, have an adult give it a stir. The sugar makes the mixture really hot, and sometimes the berries pop and splatter.

4. Take the saucepan off the heat and stir in the remaining 1 cup berries. Set aside to cool.

5. While the mixture is cooling, put 1 piecrust in the pie plate. You don't want to stretch it or it will shrink, so sort of drape it over the edges of the plate and then smooth it out with your fingers. Pour the cooled filling into the pie plate and lay the other piecrust over the top so the edges hang down evenly all around.

6. This is the important part! Fold the bottom crust up over the top one and then pinch the crusts together with your fingers or use a fork to press down really firmly on the edges of the pie plate. Now, take the butter knife and make three or four small slits in the top crust so steam can escape while the pie **bakes**.

7. Carefully place the pie in the hot oven and bake it for 30 minutes, or until the crust is golden brown. Have an adult remove the pie from the oven and transfer it to the cooling rack. Wait about 30 minutes before digging in.

Add blueberries to the saucepan.   They'll cook down quite a bit.   Dig in!

# KALBI BEEF

## You'll Need:

- One 3-inch piece fresh ginger, grated
- 2 pounds beef short ribs
- 2 cups soy sauce, preferably low sodium
- 3/4 cup firmly packed light brown sugar
- 3/4 cup granulated sugar
- 1/2 cup sliced scallions

- 1/2 cup **chopped** red onion
- 2 tablespoons black sesame seeds (see Note)
- 1-1/2 teaspoons freshly ground black pepper
- 2 tablespoons extra virgin olive oil
- 2 tablespoons sesame oil
- 4 cups water

## Equipment:

- Measuring cups and spoons
- Large rectangular or oval baking dish (13 by 9 inches)
- Large bowl (4 quarts)
- Large metal or wooden spoon
- Plastic wrap
- Barbecue grill or hibachi
- Tongs
- 2 large plates, 1 for serving

Lay ribs in a baking dish.

Pour the marinade over the meat.

Ono! (That's Hawaiian for "delicious!")

 # Kalbi Beef {Makes 4 servings}

1. Lay the short ribs in one flat layer in the baking dish.

2. Put the ginger, soy sauce, both sugars, scallions, red onion, sesame seeds, pepper, and both oils in the large bowl. With the spoon, stir until the sugars dissolve. Add the water, stir again, and you have just made a marinade!

3. Carefully pour the marinade over the short ribs in the dish. Cover tightly with plastic wrap and ask an adult to help you put it in the refrigerator; the dish is heavy now. Let the ribs sit in the marinade for at least an hour, but they're much better if they **marinate** overnight.

4. Have your Opa or another adult start the barbecue grill. Stay away from the grill because it's very, very hot. When the grill is hot and ready for cooking, take the ribs out of the refrigerator and use tongs to transfer them to a plate. Throw out the marinade because it has done its job.

5. Have the adult grill the ribs until they are **browned** and cooked through, about 8 minutes on each side. After the ribs have a brown crust on each side, move them to a cooler part of the grill to let them cook slowly, about 5 more minutes.

6. When they are done (no longer pink in the center), arrange the ribs on a clean serving plate (not the plate the raw meat was on) and eat them while they are juicy and hot.

NOTE: Sesame seeds and sesame oil are available in some supermarkets, in Asian grocery stores, or online.

"This is one of Opa's favorite recipes. He's our grandfather who lives in Hawaii, where there are people of all different backgrounds and cultures. This is his recipe for a traditional Korean dish." —Liv

# WIENER WEENIE DOGS

"Eating the dogs is fun, but don't look at the face first— too sad! Take them apart from the back." —Belle

## You'll Need:

- 1 package (8 ounces) refrigerated crescent dough
- 6 ready-to-eat (fully cooked) turkey hot dogs
- Sweet or dill midget pickles
- 1 red bell pepper
- Cherry tomatoes
- Pitted black olives
- Cream cheese

## Equipment:

- Cookie sheet (about 16 by 14 inches)
- Butter knife
- Wooden toothpicks
- Kitchen scissors or shears

 # Wiener Weenie Dogs {Makes 4 dogs}

1. Preheat the oven to 350° F.

2. Carefully unwrap the crescent dough. You want to try to keep two triangles together to make one long rectangle.

3. Lay the rectangle down on a clean counter. Put a hot dog on the dough and wrap the dough around it, pressing the edges together. Move it to the cookie sheet. Do this for 4 weenie dogs, saving 2 for later.

4. Cut the 2 hot dogs into thirds, and save the 4 rounded ends for the dogs' noses. Put the 4 noses on the cookie sheet, too, and **bake** for 12 to 15 minutes, or until the dough on the wrapped hot dogs is **browned** on the edges.

5. While the dogs are in the oven, prepare their legs and tails. For each dog, cut 2 pickles in half horizontally with the butter knife and carefully push a toothpick halfway into the cut end of each one. Choose another pickle for the tail and stick a toothpick in it, too.

6. Cut the red bell pepper into teardrop shapes for the floppy ears. Push a toothpick through the middle of a cherry tomato and stick the ears onto each side of the toothpick, kind of hanging down.

7. When the dogs come out of the oven, let them cool a little on the sheet, and then stick on the noses with a toothpick. With another toothpick, add a tomato head with its droopy ears. Push the toothpicks holding the legs and tails into the dogs. Last of all, cut the olives into thick squares for the eyes. Use cream cheese to stick them on.

8. Now, the fun part. Admire the dogs, and then chow down. Make sure you remove the toothpicks first!

Flatten the dough.

Roll your weenie up.

Make him doggone cute!

Carefully cut the avocado into chunks.

Arrange tomatoes.

Finish off this colorful salad.

## You'll Need:

- 1-1/2 cups corn kernels, drained if canned or thawed if frozen
- 2 cups **chopped** fresh tomatoes or halved cherry tomatoes
- 1/2 cup sliced pitted black olives
- 1 ripe avocado, scooped out and peeled, pit removed, and flesh cut into 1/2-inch chunks
- 1 ounce goat cheese, crumbled (1/4 cup)
- Your favorite salad dressing

## Equipment:

- Measuring cups and spoons
- Shallow bowl (about 1-1/2 quarts)
- Individual serving plates
- Serving spoon

# End-of-Summer Salad

{Makes 4 salads}

1. Spread out the corn in one layer in the bottom of the bowl. This will make up the base of the salad.

2. Make a ring of tomatoes around the outside edges of the bowl. Next, make a ring of olives inside the ring of tomatoes. Finally, put the avocado chunks in the middle and sprinkle the goat cheese over the top. Isn't this salad pretty?

3. Spoon the salad onto individual plates and have everyone put on their own dressing. You need just a little dressing because this salad already has lots of flavor.

"I love tomatoes, especially cherry tomatoes. One time, I ate all the tomatoes before we even got to the part in the recipe where we needed them! Now Mama and Miss Gaylon have to hide them from me during our shoots." —Liv

# STRAWBERRY ROSEBUDS

"These are so cute—from far away, they really look like roses, but you can eat them! We love them for any special occasion, like a birthday or our parents' anniversary. If you use them as table decorations at a party, you could say, 'Hey—let's eat the flowers!'" —Liv

Arrange celery stalks in bud vase.

Trim the "stems" of your roses.

Carefully place your "rose-buds" on their stems.

## You'll Need:

- 2 big celery stalks with some pretty leafy tops
- 2 long bamboo skewers
- 2 big strawberries with their green tops left on

## Equipment:

- Bud vase with a wide mouth (these are usually tall and skinny)
- Kitchen scissors or shears

# Strawberry Rosebuds

{Makes 1 rosebud bouquet}

**1.** Fill the vase about half full of water. This will help keep it from tipping over and keep the celery fresh, too.

**2.** Put the celery stalks in the vase with the leafy parts sticking out.

**3.** Cut about 1 inch off the bottom of one of the skewers so the stems for the "rosebuds" (the strawberries) will be different lengths, just as if they were real flowers.

**4.** Starting with the green top, carefully push each strawberry into the pointy end of a skewer. Put each skewer in the vase. Doesn't this look like a pretty flower bouquet? The best part is that you get to eat it.

*Honey takes forever! Be patient.*

*Mince the garlic.*

*A funnel helps here.*

## You'll Need:

- 1 cup ketchup
- 1/2 cup white vinegar
- 3 tablespoons honey
- 3 garlic cloves, peeled
- Pinch of freshly ground black pepper

## Equipment:

- Measuring cups and spoons
- Medium bowl (about 3 quarts)
- Large metal or wooden spoon for stirring
- Funnel, optional
- Jar for storing, optional

# Belle's Bestest BBQ Sauce {Makes 1 pint of sauce}

1. Pour the ketchup, vinegar, and honey into the bowl.

2. Finely **chop** the garlic into tiny pieces, which is called mincing. Because this is done with a sharp knife, it is best to get an adult to do it for you. Add the garlic to the sauce, along with the black pepper.

3. The barbecue sauce is now ready to pour over chicken, ribs, hamburgers, or even tofu before you cook it. If you don't use it up right away, pour it through the funnel that is set in the mouth of the jar. Cover and refrigerate for up to 1 week.

"If I have leftover barbecue sauce, I like to put it in a jar with a label on it that says BELLE'S BESTEST BBQ SAUCE. The next time we need it, it's ready. You could also give it as a gift—just don't give away the recipe!" —Belle

"This pie recipe is from our friends Cody, Taylor, and Sabrina—it's their grandma's favorite recipe. I think it tastes a lot like pumpkin pie, but try it for yourself." —Belle

## You'll Need:

• 3 medium sweet potatoes
• 4 tablespoons (1/2 stick) unsalted butter
• 1/2 cup sugar
• 2 large eggs
• 1 can (14 ounces) sweetened condensed milk
• 1 tablespoon ground cinnamon
• 1 tablespoon ground nutmeg
• 1 teaspoon pure vanilla extract
• 2 frozen 9-inch pie shells, thawed

## Equipment:

• Measuring cups and spoons
• Large bowl (about 4 quarts)
• Wooden spoon for mashing and stirring
• Hand mixer
• Cooling rack

 # Sweet Potato Pie

{Makes 6 to 8 servings}

1. Preheat the oven to 400° F.

2. **Bake** the sweet potatoes for about 50 minutes, or until they are very soft.

3. Take the potatoes out and turn down the oven temperature to 350° F.

4. Scrape the flesh from the cooked potatoes and put it in the bowl (be careful, the skins are hot). Add the butter so it starts to melt. Add the sugar and start to mash up the potatoes with the wooden spoon.

5. Add the eggs and keep mashing a little bit. Stir in the sweetened condensed milk. (This is the sticky-sweet condensed milk in a can, not evaporated milk.)

6. Next, add the cinnamon, nutmeg, and vanilla, and stir to blend. Doesn't it smell good?

7. Use the hand mixer to combine all the ingredients together until fairly smooth. This may take a few minutes to get the lumps out. Pour the mixture into the two pie shells and carefully put the pies in the oven.

8. Bake the pies for 45 minutes, or until the edges are golden brown and the center is set.

9. When ready, have an adult take the pies out of the oven and place them on a rack to cool for at least 30 minutes before eating. Do you think it tastes like pumpkin pie, too?

Scoop the potato from the skins.

Add eggs.

Your family's gonna love this!

# BERRY DIP & ROLL

Add cinnamon to brown sugar.

Dip in the sour cream.

Roll in the sugar and pop in your mouth!

## You'll Need:

- 1 pint fresh strawberries
- 1/2 cup firmly packed light brown sugar
- 1-1/2 teaspoons ground cinnamon
- 1 cup sour cream

## Equipment:

- Measuring cups and spoons
- 3 small bowls (about 1 quart each)
- Fork
- Large serving plate or platter

# Berry Dip & Roll

{Makes 2 to 4 servings}

1. Wash and drain the strawberries and remove the stems and leaves.

2. Put the brown sugar in one of the bowls. Add the cinnamon and blend the mixture with the fork. Put the sour cream in the other bowl.

3. Now, the fun part. Roll a strawberry in the sour cream, lift it up, then dip it all over in the brown sugar. Place it on a pretty serving plate and repeat until all the strawberries are dipped. Eat them while they are still cold.

"Tastes just like strawberry cheesecake: heavenly. You can take it on a picnic and put each of the ingredients in a plastic bowl with a lid. When it's time for dessert, you just dip and roll!" —Liv

# RECIPE NOTES

......................................................................................................................

......................................................................................................................

......................................................................................................................

......................................................................................................................

......................................................................................................................

......................................................................................................................

......................................................................................................................

......................................................................................................................

......................................................................................................................

......................................................................................................................

......................................................................................................................

......................................................................................................................

......................................................................................................................

......................................................................................................................

......................................................................................................................

......................................................................................................................

......................................................................................................................

Fabulous Fall
Recipes!

Ghosts in the Graveyard Meat Loaf

Black Bean Chili

Stumpkins

# FALL

"The really cool part of this recipe is decorating the meatloaf with the gravestones. Make sure the hole you cut in the corner of your plastic bag is teeny—otherwise you won't be able to write spooky messages on your gravestone with blood. I mean ketchup." —Liv

Gather all your ingredients together.

Mix meat, veggies and ketchup with eggs.

Pat into a baking pan.

## You'll Need:

- 1-1/2 pounds lean ground beef or turkey
- 3/4 cup finely **chopped** onion
- 1/2 cup ketchup
- 1/3 cup dried bread crumbs
- 1/3 cup finely chopped or grated carrots
- 1/4 cup chopped dill pickles
- 1 tablespoon Dijon mustard
- 1 to 2 garlic cloves, peeled and finely chopped
- 2 large eggs
- 1 loaf of long skinny French bread (called a baguette)
- Extra virgin olive oil
- Curly kale leaves
- 1 recipe Mashed Potato Ghosts (page 78)

## Equipment:

- Measuring cups and spoons
- Large bowl (about 4 quarts)
- Large metal or wooden spoon
- 13- by 9-inch loaf pan
- Nonstick vegetable cooking spray
- Pastry brush
- Cookie sheet (about 16 by 14 inches)
- Plastic sandwich bag
- Large serving plate or platter
- Metal spatula

 # Ghosts in the Graveyard Meat Loaf

{Makes 8 servings}

**1.** While the oven is cold, move one of the racks to the lower third of the oven (for the meat loaf) and one to the upper third (for the bread). Preheat the oven to 350° F.

**2.** Put the meat, onion, ketchup, bread crumbs, carrots, pickles, mustard, garlic, and eggs into the bowl. Mix up the ingredients with your hands. Isn't it fun to squish the eggs before you mix them into the meat? Remember to wash your hands with soap and water before touching anything else. If you don't like to mix things with your hands, use the big spoon.

**3.** Spray the inside of the loaf pan with the cooking spray. Press the meat mixture into the pan, spreading and smoothing it as you go.

**4.** Put the pan on the bottom rack of the oven and **bake** until it gets a nice **brown** crust, 35 to 40 minutes.

**5.** Meanwhile, have an adult cut off the ends of the bread diagonally, and then slice off eight 1/2-inch diagonal pieces. Using the pastry brush, brush both sides of the bread slices with the olive oil and put them on the cookie sheet.

**6.** Put some ketchup into a small plastic sandwich bag and seal it shut. Cut off one of the corners on a diagonal, but make sure the cut is very tiny. Now squeeze the bag like a pastry bag to make the letters RIP ("rest in peace") on the bread.

**7.** Place the cookie sheet on the top rack of the oven. Bake for about 4 minutes, or until the edges of the bread are toasted and beginning to get brown. Have an adult take the sheet out of the oven; let the "gravestones" cool.

**8.** When the meat loaf is done, have an adult help you take it out of the oven. Turn the loaf out of the pan onto the large platter. Cut into eight pieces. Push one gravestone into the meat at one end of each piece of meat loaf. (If the gravestone doesn't stand up by itself, you can use some of the leftover mashed potatoes from the ghosts to hold it up.)

**9.** Arrange some of the curly kale around the "graves." Use the spatula to place a Mashed Potato Ghost on each grave.

## You'll Need:

- 8 large red potatoes
- 1/2 cup whole milk
- 4 ounces white Cheddar cheese, shredded (1 cup)
- 16 whole olives, pitted and cut into quarters

## Equipment:

- Large saucepan (4 to 6 quarts)
- Colander
- Potato masher or hand mixer
- Large plastic resealable storage bag
- Kitchen scissors or shears
- Parchment paper
- Cookie sheet (about 16 to 14 inches)
- Big metal spatula

Mash the potatoes.

Cut the tip of the bag off.

Use the bag to squeeze out your ghosts!

# Mashed Potato Ghosts

{Makes 8 ghosts}

1. Scrub and peel the potatoes and rinse them in cold water.

2. Put the potatoes in the saucepan and fill with water until it covers the potatoes. Place the pan over high heat and bring the water to a **boil**. Turn down the heat and **simmer** the potatoes until they are very tender, about 35 minutes.

3. Have an adult dump the potatoes into a colander to drain and then put them back into the same pan. Pour in the milk and start smashing the potatoes with the potato masher.

4. Add the cheese while the mashed potatoes are still hot. Continue to smash them some more so the cheese starts to melt a little and is well mixed into the potatoes.

5. By this time, the potatoes won't be as hot, so spoon them into the plastic bag and close it tightly. Cut off one bottom corner of the bag, making a 1/2-inch opening.

6. Lay one sheet of parchment paper on the cookie sheet. This is the really fun part. Squeeze the bag so the potatoes will come out in a long tube onto the parchment paper (this is called piping). Start by making a circle about 1-1/2 inches across. Then squeeze out more potatoes on top of the circle to make a ghost shape. After you make 8 ghosts, stick 3 olive pieces into each of their heads for "eyes and a mouth."

7. When you take the toast gravestones out of the oven (page 77), put the ghosts in and **bake** them for about 7 minutes, or until they get hot. Have an adult take the ghosts out of the oven. Use the spatula to transfer the ghosts to their "graves" (the meat loaf pieces).

"Boys and ghouls—
this is a great recipe if you're
having friends over for a Halloween
dinner. When you make the Mashed Potato
Ghosts, do them while the spuds are still
warm—that's important for shaping
your little Casper." —Belle

# ROOT VEGETABLE BAKE

"You might not turn up for turnips on their own, but for this dish you'll come running to the table. No, I'm not kidding." —Belle

Check out other harvest-time recipes at www.spatulatta.com

## You'll Need:

- 1 large turnip
- 1 large parsnip
- 1 large sweet potato
- 5 or 6 very small onions
- 1 cup baby carrots (16 to 18 carrots)
- 1 tablespoon kosher (coarse) salt
- 1/4 cup canned chicken or vegetable broth, preferably low sodium

## Equipment:

- Large casserole dish (about 3-1/2 quarts)
- Large metal or wooden spoon

 # Root Vegetable Bake {Makes 6 servings}

**1.** Preheat the oven to 350° F.

**2.** Have an adult peel the turnip, parsnip, and sweet potato and cut each into 1-inch chunks. Meanwhile, peel the onions.

**3.** Put the cut-up vegetables and the carrots and onions into the bottom of the casserole dish. Sprinkle the salt over the vegetables and then pour in the broth.

**4.** Use the spoon (or even your hands, if you want to) to mix up the vegetables so they get nicely coated with the broth.

**5.** Put the casserole dish in the oven and **bake** for 1 hour. Ask the adult to stir the vegetables every 20 minutes to coat them with the broth again. When the edges of the vegetables start to get brown, poke them with a fork to see if they are soft and tender. That means they are done.

This is a turnip and a parsnip.

Coat the veggies with broth.

Place in the oven to bake.

## You'll Need:

- 3 tablespoons vegetable oil, such as canola
- 1 cup coarsely **chopped** onions
- 1/2 cup chopped red or green bell pepper (the sweet kind)
- 2 garlic cloves, peeled and finely chopped
- 1 pound ground turkey (see Note)

- 2 tablespoons chili powder
- 1 tablespoon ground cumin
- 1 tablespoon dried oregano
- 2 cans (16 ounces each) black beans, rinsed and drained
- 1 can (28 ounces) whole tomatoes with their juices (don't drain them)

## Equipment:

- Measuring cups and spoons
- Large soup pot or stockpot (about 8 quarts)
- Large metal or wooden spoon for stirring
- Kitchen scissors or shears
- Ladle
- Individual soup bowls

Add beans to the meat mixture.

Use kitchen scissors to cut tomatoes into bite-sized chunks.

# Black Bean Chili

{Makes 4 to 6 servings}

1. Pour the oil into the pot and heat for about 2 minutes. Add the onions, red peppers, and garlic. **Sauté** over medium heat until the onions are transparent. This will take about 5 minutes.

2. Add the ground turkey, then sprinkle in the chili powder, cumin, and oregano.

3. Break up the turkey with your spoon and let it **brown**. Keep stirring and breaking up the turkey so the little clumps of meat get brown on all sides.

4. Next, pour the black beans and tomatoes into the pot. Give it all a good stir. Here's a tip: Keep the tomato can close to the inside of the pot while you pour in the tomatoes and their juices—so they don't splash on you. Use the scissors or shears to break up the tomatoes into chunks.

5. Cook over medium-high heat until the liquid gets bubbly. Then turn down the heat so the chili **simmers,** but doesn't **boil.** Simmer for about 40 minutes, stirring every once in a while, until the chili thickens.

6. Ladle the chili into individual bowls and enjoy!

NOTE: If you don't want to put meat in your chili, you can substitute meatless crumbles, which you'll find frozen at your supermarket. And you don't even have to thaw them out first.

"This chili is perfect for a fall day. Its flavor gets even better the next day, so if you have any left over, you can pour it into a thermos to take to school for lunch." —Liv

Check out other lunch ideas at www.spatulatta.com

"This is really tasty. When you use a slow cooker, you can make dinner in the morning and forget about it! Then when you get home from skating or swimming or drama—it's ready to eat." —Belle

## You'll Need:

- 1 bottle (12 ounces) chili sauce
- 1 cup firmly packed dark brown sugar
- 1 large red onion, coarsely **chopped**
- 1/4 cup cider vinegar
- 7 garlic cloves, peeled and finely chopped
- 1 tablespoon chili powder
- 1 tablespoon Worcestershire sauce
- 1 teaspoon liquid smoke (see Note)
- One 3-pound boneless pork shoulder roast
- Buns or rolls for serving

## Equipment:

- Measuring cups and spoons
- Large bowl (about 4 quarts)
- Large metal or wooden spoon for stirring and mixing
- Slow cooker
- 2 forks

 # Pulled Pork Sandwiches {Makes 10 to 12 sandwiches}

1. Combine all of the ingredients except the pork in the bowl.

2. Use the spoon to stir and mix them to make a nice thick sauce.

3. Put the pork in the slow cooker. Pour the sauce over it and close the lid of the cooker.

4. Set the heat to low, and let the pork cook until it is very, very tender, about 8 hours.

5. This is the cool part. Use the 2 forks to pull the pork into little pieces, then mix the pork with the sauce. Guess where the title of this recipe came from?

6. Now, spoon the pulled pork onto your favorite buns or rolls and enjoy! But make sure to have plenty of napkins handy. (In the unlikely event that you have leftovers or want to make it ahead, pulled pork freezes really well.)

NOTE: Liquid smoke is something you can buy in a bottle and is available at most supermarkets.

Patience...

Measure ingredients and put into the bowl.

Pour sauce over the meat.

# CRUNCHY CHICKEN YAKITORI

## You'll Need:

- 1/4 cup soy sauce, preferably low sodium
- 3 garlic cloves, peeled and finely **chopped**
- 1-inch piece fresh gingerroot, grated or very finely chopped (see Note)
- 1 tablespoon honey
- 1/2 teaspoon sesame oil
- 1 pound boneless, skinless chicken breast halves, cut into 1-inch strips
- 2 cups cornflakes

## Equipment:

- Measuring cups and spoons
- 12-inch bamboo skewers
- Shallow pan
- Medium bowl (about 3 quarts)
- Large metal or wooden spoon for stirring
- 2 large resealable plastic storage bags
- Rolling pin, optional
- Flat plate
- Cookie sheet (about 16 by 14 inches)
- Aluminum foil

Pour marinade onto the chicken strips.

Carefully thread chicken onto skewers.

# Crunchy Chicken Yakitori

{Makes 4 to 6 servings}

**1.** Lay the bamboo skewers in a shallow pan and pour cold water over them. Let them soak for about an hour. This is so they won't burn in the oven later on.

**2.** Combine the soy sauce, garlic, gingerroot, honey, and sesame oil in the bowl. Stir until the honey disappears. This is the marinade.

**3.** Pour the marinade into one of the plastic bags. Add the chicken breasts and close the bag tightly. Gently shake the bag until all the chicken is coated with the marinade. Put the bag in the refrigerator for 30 minutes.

**4.** Preheat the oven to 350° F.

**5.** Put the cornflakes in the other plastic bag. Use your hands or a rolling pin to crush the cereal. Don't make the pieces too small. Pour the crumbs onto the plate or another shallow container.

**6.** After the chicken has **marinated** for 30 minutes, take the bag out of the refrigerator, hold it over the sink, open the bag just a tiny bit, and pour out the marinade.

**7.** Next, thread the chicken strips onto the skewers. This is sort of like weaving. Holding up the pointy part of a skewer (be careful—it is very sharp), push one end of a chicken strip onto the skewer. Move the chicken strip down a little and then push the skewer through it again. Repeat this until you have covered most of the skewer with chicken. Leave enough room on the bottom so you have a "handle."

8. Roll the skewered chicken in the cornflake crumbs. Gently pat the crumbs onto any of the chicken that doesn't get covered.

9. Cover the cookie sheet with aluminum foil. Place the chicken skewers on the foil so all the handles are in a line. Take another piece of foil and cover the ends of the skewers so they don't burn.

10. Place the sheet in the oven and **bake** until the chicken is cooked through and golden brown, about 10 minutes. Pull the chicken off the skewers with your fingers or eat it straight off the skewer.

NOTE: Gingerroot is available in most supermarkets and in Asian grocery stores.

"We call them stick pumpkins, or stumpkins. But really, they are sweet pumpkin-flavored cookies baked on a stick and decorated like a jack-o'-lantern, or a spooky monster—your choice."
—Liv

Mix ingredients together.

Pat into molds.

Decorate how the spirits move you.

## You'll Need:
- 8 tablespoons (1 stick) unsalted butter, softened (see Note)
- 1 cup firmly packed light brown sugar
- 1/2 cup granulated sugar
- 1 large egg
- 1 teaspoon pure vanilla extract
- 2 teaspoons pumpkin pie spice
- 2-1/2 cups all-purpose flour
- 1 teaspoon baking soda
- 2 tubes cake decorating icing, preferably orange and green
- Pieces of candy corn and black licorice

## Equipment:
- Measuring cups and spoons
- Medium bowl (about 3 quarts)
- Hand mixer
- "Cookie pop" pan with slots for sticks
- Nonstick vegetable cooking spray
- Lollipop sticks
- Cooling rack
- Plastic sandwich storage bags (with fold-down tops)
- Ribbon
- Kitchen scissors or shears

 # Stumpkins {Makes 10 to 12 stumpkins}

1. Preheat the oven to 350° F.

2. Put the softened butter and the two sugars in the bowl. Blend with the hand mixer on medium speed until they get fluffy. This is called **creaming** the butter and sugar.

3. Add the egg and vanilla and **beat** to combine. Add the pumpkin spice and beat again until well combined. Add the flour and baking soda and mix at low speed (so the flour doesn't fly out of the bowl). The batter should be pretty thick.

4. Spray the cookie pop pan with the cooking spray. Lay the sticks in place, almost to the top of each round depression.

5. Spoon 3 generous tablespoonfuls of batter into each depression. Pat down to fill the mold. Jiggle the stick around so it is in the middle of the batter.

6. **Bake** for 12 to 15 minutes, or until the top springs back when it's touched (have an adult do this part). The stumpkins should be a bit puffy.

7. This is important. Let the stumpkins cool all the way in the pan on a rack before taking them out of the pan.

8. Make a jack-o-lantern face on the stumpkins with icing; stick on candy corn or licorice bits.

9. Once the icing has set, slide each stumpkin into a plastic sandwich bag. Close the bag by tying it with a ribbon right underneath the stumpkin and making a bow. Now you have a special treat for friends or to use as Halloween party favors!

NOTE: Before using it, get the butter out of the refrigerator and let it stand on the counter for 30 minutes so it isn't so hard. Or, if you are in a hurry, you can put the cold stick of butter in the microwave oven and zap it on high for 10 or 12 seconds to soften it a little. Softening makes it easier to mix the butter with the sugars.

# HARVEST SOUP

## You'll Need:

- 1 medium butternut squash
- 3 to 4 tablespoons extra virgin olive oil
- 1/2 cup finely **chopped** onion
- 1 large carrot cut in 1-inch chunks
- 1/2 teaspoon dried rosemary leaves

- 4 cups chicken stock or canned low-sodium chicken broth, heated
- 1/4 cup coarsely chopped smoked almonds

## Equipment:

- Measuring cups and spoons
- Large soup pot or stockpot (about 8 quarts)
- Large slotted spoon
- Food processor
- Ladle
- Individual soup bowls

*Squash and carrots give this soup it's beautiful fall color.*

*Sprinkle almonds onto soup before serving.*

## Harvest Soup {Makes 6 to 8 servings}

1. Have an adult peel and cut the squash into 1-inch chunks. The squash is very hard and it takes a big sharp knife to cut it up.

2. Pour the oil into the bottom of the pot. Add the onion and stir over medium heat until the onion is translucent (see-through), 3 to 4 minutes.

3. Add the squash, carrots, and rosemary to the pot. Have an adult pour the hot chicken stock into the pot. Having hot stock gives the soup a head start on cooking.

4. Cook until the vegetables are very soft and tender, 25 to 30 minutes. Check the vegetables with a fork or knife to test for tenderness.

5. When the vegetables are done, have an adult move the pot close to the food processor. Use the slotted spoon to scoop up some of the vegetables, letting the stock drain. Put them into the food processor. Continue until the bowl of the food processor is about half full. (If you have too many vegetables, it takes a long time to get them smooth, so do it in two batches.)

6. Process the first batch of vegetables. When the mixture looks smooth and has no more lumps (this is called **pureeing**), stop the food processor. If the vegetables aren't getting pureed, add a little more broth from the pot. They may need some more liquid to get smooth.

7. Once the vegetables are pureed, add enough of the stock to make the soup as thin or as thick as you like. Process to mix again. Carefully ladle the soup into the soup bowls. Sprinkle almonds over each bowl and serve immediately.

"This is one of the prettiest soups you'll ever make. One time we served it in a hollowed-out little pumpkin shell—everybody loved it that way." —Belle

# BOSS BANANA BREAD

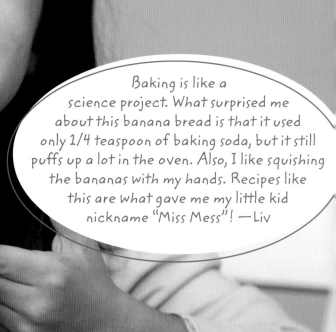

Baking is like a science project. What surprised me about this banana bread is that it used only 1/4 teaspoon of baking soda, but it still puffs up a lot in the oven. Also, I like squishing the bananas with my hands. Recipes like this are what gave me my little kid nickname "Miss Mess"! —Liv

## You'll Need:

- 8 tablespoons (1 stick) unsalted butter, softened
- 1 cup sugar
- 2 bananas, mashed
- 2 large eggs
- 2 cups all-purpose flour
- 1/4 teaspoon baking soda
- 1/4 teaspoon salt

## Equipment:

- Loaf pan (about 9 by 4 inches)
- Nonstick vegetable cooking spray
- Large bowl (about 4 quarts)
- Hand mixer
- Rubber spatula
- Cooling rack

 # Boss Banana Bread {Makes 1 loaf banana bread}

1. Preheat the oven to 350° F. Spray the loaf pan with the cooking spray.

2. In the large bowl with the hand mixer, **cream** together the butter and the sugar until light yellow. All the air you **beat** into the mix makes it fluffier.

3. Add the mashed-up bananas and the eggs. Mix well to combine.

4. Add the flour, baking soda, and salt and mix well. You can do this part by hand with the spatula if you want to, but you can also use the mixer.

5. Scrape the batter into your loaf pan with the spatula.

6. **Bake** for 1 hour, or until a tester inserted into the center comes out clean.

7. Remove the pan from the oven and let cool for about 15 minutes before turning it out onto a cooling rack. Enjoy the delicious smells in your kitchen! A little pat of butter on a slice is heaven.

*Cream the butter and sugar.*

*Mash the bananas.*

*Use a spatula when you pour the batter.*

# RECIPE NOTES

..................................................................................................................
..................................................................................................................
..................................................................................................................
..................................................................................................................
..................................................................................................................
..................................................................................................................
..................................................................................................................
..................................................................................................................
..................................................................................................................
..................................................................................................................
..................................................................................................................
..................................................................................................................
..................................................................................................................
..................................................................................................................
..................................................................................................................
..................................................................................................................
..................................................................................................................

FALL 94

V E G E T A R I A N

Yummy
Vegetarian
Recipes!

Spatulatta Enchilada

My Big Fat Greek Salad

Millet & Chickpea Salad

# VEGETARIAN

"This is a little bit different from the regular old three-bean salad. It tastes best if you can leave it in the fridge for a couple hours, or even overnight. It's great in a thermos for lunch at school, too." —Liv

Check out more vegetarian recipes at www.spatulatta.com

## You'll Need:

- 1 can (15.5 ounces) chickpeas (also called garbanzo beans)
- 1 can (15.5 ounces) kidney beans
- 1 can (15.5 ounces) cannellini beans
- 1/2 red onion, finely **chopped**
- 2 celery stalks, finely chopped
- 1/2 cup finely chopped fresh parsley

Dressing

- 1/3 cup extra virgin olive oil
- 1/3 cup apple cider vinegar
- 1/3 cup sugar
- 1-1/2 teaspoons salt
- 1/2 teaspoon freshly ground black pepper

## Equipment:

- Measuring cups and spoons
- Can opener
- Large colander
- Medium bowl (about 3 quarts)
- Large metal or wooden spoon for stirring
- 4-cup Pyrex measuring cup
- Whisk

 # Blue Ribbon Bean Salad

{Makes 6 bean salads}

1. Use the can opener to open the cans of beans.

2. Empty the beans into the colander and rinse and drain them.

3. Place the drained beans in the medium bowl. Add the chopped onion, celery, and parsley and stir well. Set aside.

4. In the measuring cup, combine the oil, vinegar, sugar, salt, and pepper and **whisk** to mix well to make the dressing.

5. Pour the dressing over the salad and stir to combine. It's extra good if you let it sit awhile!

Open the beans.

Mix the dressing.

Pour over salad and mix again.

# CHEESE BOEREG

Lay half the phyllo sheets in pan.

Pour cheese mixture into pan.

Pour milk and butter over the whole pan.

## You'll Need:

- 1 pound Muenster or brick cheese, shredded (about 4 cups)
- 1 pound feta cheese, crumbled
- 1/2 cup **chopped** fresh dill
- 2 large eggs
- 1 package (8 ounces) frozen phyllo dough, thawed
- 1-1/2 cups 2% milk
- 8 to 12 tablespoons (1 to 1-1/2 sticks) unsalted butter, melted (see Note)

## Equipment:

- Measuring cups and spoons
- 13- by 9-inch baking pan
- Nonstick vegetable cooking spray
- Large bowl (about 4 quarts)
- Large metal or wooden spoon for stirring
- Small bowl (about 1-1/2 quarts)
- Fork
- Cutting board
- Kitchen scissors or shears
- Flat spatula (about 10 inches) or flat-blade knife
- 4-cup Pyrex measuring cup

# Cheese Boereg {Makes 12 servings}

1. Place the two cheeses in the large bowl and stir to combine. Stir in the dill.

2. Carefully break the eggs into the small bowl. **Beat** the eggs with a fork, then add them to the cheese mixture. Set aside.

3. Coat the baking pan with the nonstick cooking spray.

4. Gently place the sheets of phyllo dough on a cutting board, counter, or other clean hard surface. Make sure the widest side faces you. Fold the dough vertically in half as if it were a book. Have an adult help you cut along the fold with the scissors or shears. Lift up half of the sheets and lay them neatly in the bottom of the baking pan.

5. Spread the cheese mixture over the phyllo dough, making sure it reaches all the way to the edges.

6. Have an adult help you slice the boereg in the pan into twelve 3-inch squares: Cut through the cheese and layers of phyllo, all the way to the bottom of the pan.

7. Add the milk to the melted butter. Stir well.

8. Pour the milk and butter mixture over the entire pan. You want to moisten the top layer of phyllo and let the milk seep all the way down through the cuts. Let the pan sit for 1 to 3 hours in the refrigerator. This "rest" is important so that the phyllo can soak up the milk and butter.

"We used a fork to crumble the feta on our marble countertop. But we didn't realize we were gouging it. So make sure that when you use a hard or sharp object on your counter, put a cutting board on the counter first, so you can stay out of trouble with your mother!" —Belle

**9.** When you are ready to proceed, preheat the oven to 350° F.

**10.** Place the baking pan in the oven and **bake** for 45 minutes to 1 hour, or until the top is crispy and golden brown.  Yes, it does taste as good as it looks!

NOTE:  Put the butter in a 4-cup Pyrex measuring cup. **Microwave** on high for 60 seconds until melted.

"This is a good recipe to make when you have lots of veggies (even leftovers) in the fridge. Putting the enchiladas in the pan is a little bit tricky, but if you just turn over the tortillas so the folded edge is on the bottom, they'll stay together."
—Liv

## You'll Need:

- 1 can (14 ounces) black beans, rinsed and drained
- 1 can (4.5 ounces) **chopped** green chiles
- 1 cup thinly sliced red onions
- 2 celery stalks, cleaned and finely chopped
- 1 red or yellow bell pepper, cut into strips
- 1 package (10 ounces) frozen corn kernels, thawed
- 3/4 cup sliced black olives
- Twelve 8-inch corn tortillas
- 1 can (14 ounces) enchilada sauce
- 2 cups shredded Cheddar cheese

## Equipment:

- Measuring cups and spoons
- Medium bowl (about 3 quarts)
- Soup spoon
- 13- by 9-inch baking dish

# Spatulatta Enchilada {Makes 12 enchiladas}

1. Preheat the oven to 350° F.

2. In a large skillet on medium heat, mix the beans, chiles, onions, celery, corn, olives, and peppers together. We're just warming the veggies a little. Remove from heat and place the skillet on a trivet next to your baking dish.

3. Place 1 corn tortilla on a counter or other flat surface and add a couple of generous spoonfuls of the veggies into the center.

4. Starting from an edge, roll the tortilla into a tube shape, carefully turn the tortilla roll upside down, and place it in the baking dish. Continue filling and rolling the enchiladas and placing them right next to each other in the dish.

5. When all of the enchiladas are in the pan, pour the enchilada sauce and cover them with a layer of cheese.

6. Place the dish in the oven and cook until heated through, 25 to 30 minutes. Serve and enjoy!

Put veggies in the skillet.  Roll tortilla into a tube.  Pour sauce over the enchiladas.

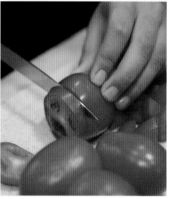

Cut ripe tomatoes into chunks.

## You'll Need:

- 2 ripe red plum tomatoes
- 2 cucumbers, peeled
- 4 ounces feta cheese, crumbled
- 1/3 cup Kalamata olives
- 1/4 red onion, thinly sliced, optional
- 1/4 cup extra virgin olive oil
- 1 tablespoon red wine vinegar, optional
- 1 tablespoon dried oregano
- Salt and freshly ground black pepper to taste

## Equipment:

- Measuring cups and spoons
- Pretty serving bowl (about 2 quarts)
- Large metal or wooden spoon

# My Big Fat Greek Salad

{4 to 6 servings}

1. Cut the tomatoes and cucumbers into 1/2-inch chunks and put them in the bowl. Add the crumbled feta. Using the spoon, stir in the olives and onion slices, if using.

2. Drizzle the salad with olive oil and sprinkle with the red wine vinegar, if using. Season with the oregano, salt, and pepper. Toss and serve.

Drizzle the olive oil.

Love it!

"Even if you're just starting to work in the kitchen, this is a great salad to make for your family or friends. Our friend Peter showed us how to make it, and we love it!" —Belle

"This salad is fun to eat because it has some crunchy veggies in it. I really like the millet, which adds another neat texture because the grains kind of pop in your mouth. We made this for a friend who was allergic to wheat and dairy—he loved it." —Liv

## You'll Need:

- 3/4 cup whole millet
- 1-1/2 cups vegetable stock
- 1/2 cup canned chickpeas (also called garbanzo beans), rinsed and drained
- 1/2 cup sliced black olives
- 1/2 cup finely **chopped** red onion
- 1/2 cup finely chopped red bell pepper
- 1/4 cup balsamic vinegar
- 1/4 cup extra virgin olive oil

## Equipment:

- Measuring cups and spoons
- Small saucepan (1 to 1-1/2 quarts) with a tight-fitting lid
- Large bowl (about 4 quarts)
- Fork
- Large metal or wooden spoon for stirring
- 4-cup Pyrex measuring cup
- Whisk

 # Millet & Chickpea Salad {Makes 4 salads}

**1.** Pour the millet and vegetable stock into the saucepan, stir, and cover. Cook over medium heat until the grain is tender, about 20 minutes. (Test the millet for doneness as you would pasta.)

**2.** Remove the saucepan from the heat and fluff the millet with a fork.

**3.** Transfer the millet to the large bowl. Add the chickpeas, olives, red onion, and red bell pepper. Stir to combine.

**4.** In the measuring cup, **whisk** the vinegar and oil until well combined.

**5.** Drizzle the "dressing" over the salad. Use the fork to toss the salad until all the colorful vegetables are spread throughout. Why not pack your salad in a resealable container and take it with you to school?

Put cooked millet into a bowl.

Add the chickpeas.

Pour on the dressing.

Transfer rice from cooker to bowl.

Add mushrooms.

Snip strips of nori and sprinkle on top.

## You'll Need:

- 4 dried black mushrooms— soaked and thinly sliced
- 3 cups cooked sushi rice
- 2 tablespoons sugar
- 5 tablespoons rice wine vinegar (or cider vinegar slightly diluted with water)
- 1 cup frozen green peas, thawed, or thinly sliced fresh snow peas
- 2 tablespoons pickled ginger, cut into thin strips
- 2 inari (fried tofu skin pouches), thinly sliced
- 1 sheet nori (roasted seaweed wrapper)

## Equipment:

- Measuring cups and spoons
- Large, pretty serving bowl (about 4 quarts)
- Rice paddle or large silicon spoon
- Kitchen scissors or shears

## Sushi Rice Salad {4 to 6 servings}

1. Soak the dried black mushrooms in warm water for 1 hour. Drain prior to starting.

2. Put the rice in the serving bowl. Add the sugar and vinegar. Dip the paddle in a glass of water so the rice won't stick to it and mix the rice until the sugar crystals dissolve.

3. Add the sliced mushrooms, peas, ginger, and inari strips.

4. Dip your paddle again and gently flip the ingredients until all the colors and shapes are evenly mixed. Scoop up the rice from the bottom of the bowl to make sure you get it all mixed in.

5. For the final touch, use the scissors or shears to cut thin strips of nori over the top of the salad.

NOTE: You can find sushi rice, rice wine vinegar, pickled ginger, inari, nori, and a rice paddle in Asian markets and some supermarkets.

"I like white rice, but I don't like the way it sticks to everything when you cook it. So I use a wet rice paddle, and I wet my hands, too—it keeps the rice off of them when I'm cooking."—Liv

# TOFU SALAD

"I love the smell of ginger, and this salad has lots of it. Did you know that you measure gingerroot by the hand? And that if you want just a piece of the gingerroot, you call it a finger?" —Liv

## You'll Need:
- One 3-inch piece fresh ginger
- 1 block (10 ounces) extra-firm tofu (also called bean curd)
- 2 scallions, sliced across into thin rounds
- 2 tablespoons soy sauce, preferably low sodium

## Equipment:
- Measuring cups and spoons
- Box grater or Microplane
- 4 individual salad plates

A "hand" of ginger.

Grate the ginger.

 # Tofu Salad {Makes 4 appetizer salads}

1. Peel the outer skin off the ginger. Then use the box grater or Microplane to grate the ginger. (Grating ginger is a little tricky, so if you need help from an adult, ask for it.)

2. Slice the tofu block into thirds the long way. Then slice across it the short way, cutting the tofu into 3/4-inch cubes.

3. Divide and arrange the cubes on each of the four plates. Sprinkle the ginger and scallions over each plate. Drizzle the soy sauce over each salad and serve. Try using chopsticks—that's the way they eat this in Hawaii.

Carefully slice tofu into cubes.

..................................................................................

..................................................................................

..................................................................................

..................................................................................

..................................................................................

..................................................................................

..................................................................................

..................................................................................

..................................................................................

..................................................................................

..................................................................................

..................................................................................

..................................................................................

..................................................................................

..................................................................................

..................................................................................

..................................................................................

..................................................................................

Fruit Kebabs

Tropical Celery Boats

Instant Inari Sushi

# SNACKS

"This recipe is from our friend Janie in Kentucky. We tested it out and loved it! Make sure all of the ingredients are right in front of you when you start, because this recipe comes together really fast." —Liv

## You'll Need:

- 1 package (12 ounces) taco-flavored vegetarian crumbles (see Note) or 1 pound of ground beef
- 1 package (1.25 ounces) taco seasoning, optional

- Shredded Cheddar or Monterey Jack cheese
- 3 or 4 lettuce leaves, finely shredded
- 1 ripe red tomato, coarsely **chopped**
- 4 small bags (1 ounce each) corn chips

## Equipment:

- Microwave oven or 10-inch skillet or frying pan
- Spoon
- 3 small bowls for holding accompaniments

 # Taco-a-Go-Go {Makes 4 tacos}

1. Cut the top off the bag of vegetarian crumbles, and **microwave** it. Follow the package for directions. If you're using ground beef, season it with the taco seasoning and then **brown** it with a little olive oil in a skillet or frying pan. Make sure the meat is cooked thoroughly, then ask an adult to drain off as much grease as possible.

2. Meanwhile, put the cheese, lettuce, and tomato in individual bowls.

3. While the filling is still warm—but not too hot—spoon some into each corn chip bag.

4. Spoon a little cheese into each bag. The hot filling will melt the cheese.

5. Add some lettuce and some tomato to the top of each bag. Close the top and give the bag a couple of shakes. Your Taco-a-Go-Go is ready to eat on the run!

NOTE: Vegetarian crumbles are a soy-based meat substitute. Crumbles are typically low in fat and come in many flavors besides taco. You don't have to be a vegetarian to enjoy them!

*Crumbles go into the microwave.*

*Bag the hot crumbles.*

*Add lettuce and cheese, too!*

# FRUIT KEBABS

Cut out fruit shapes.

Carefully thread your fruit on a skewer.

Attack the snack!

## You'll Need:
- About 1 cup each of 4 fresh fruits: a melon such as watermelon, honeydew, or cantaloupe; banana; pineapple; and strawberry (any of your favorite fruit will work as long as it can stay on the skewer)

## Equipment:
- Small cookie cutters—stars, hearts, and circles work best
- Butter knife
- Small bowls, such as soup or cereal bowls
- 6- to 8-inch bamboo skewers
- Serving plate
- Plastic wrap

 # Fruit Kebabs {Makes 6 kebabs}

1. Wash the strawberries and cut off the green tops.

2. Have an adult help you cut the melon and pineapple into 1/2-inch-thick slices. Discard the rinds and peels.

3. Press cookie cutters into the melon and pineapple slices to make different shapes.

4. Peel the banana and cut it into chunks with a butter knife.

5. Put all the pieces of fruit in their own small bowls so they are easy to reach.

6. Hold up a skewer so you can see the pointy end, and very carefully, start sliding the fruit onto the skewer in any order you like. Lay the filled skewers on the serving plate—aren't they pretty? Repeat until all the fruit is gone. Cover the plate with plastic wrap and put it in the refrigerator until you are ready to serve the kebabs.

"I love to bring these kebabs for school parties. Most big people think kids all want sweets and stuff, but these are the first things to go at our school."
—Liv

# TUSCAN BEAN DIP

"Papa makes this for every party, and everyone *loves* it. We use the leftovers on Italian panini (sandwiches) instead of mayo. This recipe definitely keeps the vampires away, if you know what I mean." —Belle

Add ingredients to food processor.

Olive oil makes it smooth.

Get every last bit—
it's delish!

## You'll Need:

- 1 can (15.5 ounces) cannellini beans
- 1/4 cup extra virgin olive oil
- 3 garlic cloves, peeled
- Veggies, chips, and crackers for serving

## Equipment:

- Measuring cup
- Can opener
- Food processor
- Rubber spatula
- Serving bowl

 # Tuscan Bean Dip

{Makes 2 cups of dip }

1. Open the can of beans with the can opener.

2. Pour the beans into the bowl of the food processor, then add the olive oil and garlic. Process until the mixture is smooth.

3. Have an adult remove the blade in the food processor. Now, use the rubber spatula to scrape the mixture into the serving bowl. Serve with your favorite veggies, chips, or crackers. Yum!

Mix pineapple and cream cheese together.

Spread in a celery boat.

Add a tropical touch.

## You'll Need:

- 1 can (8 ounces) crushed pineapple, drained
- 4 celery stalks, washed and patted dry
- 3 tablespoons soft cream cheese (the kind that comes in a tub)

## Equipment:

- Measuring cups and spoons
- Can opener
- Small strainer
- Small bowl (about 1 quart)
- Rubber spatula or spoon
- Butter knife or spreader
- Medium plate
- Plastic wrap
- Paper umbrellas, optional

# Tropical Celery Boats
{Makes 4 celery boats}

1. Open the can of pineapple with the can opener. Drain the pineapple through a strainer set over a bowl. Save the juice to drink or use for something else.

2. Trim the ends and any leafy parts off the celery stalks. Cut the stalks in half across the middle.

3. Put the cream cheese in the bowl. Add the pineapple and, with the rubber spatula, mix it into the cream cheese.

4. Use the butter knife or spreader to spread the mixture into the hollows of the celery stalk halves.

5. Put the filled celery stalks on the plate and, if you aren't going to eat them right away, cover them with plastic wrap and put them in the refrigerator until you are ready to serve.

"We've made this recipe ever since I can remember. We like to stick tiny paper umbrellas into the cream cheese mixture to make the snack even more fun to eat."
—Belle and Liv

"This is a favorite snack food for children in Japan. You can find the sushi rice seasoning powder packets and the tofu pouches—inari envelopes—in Asian grocery stores." —Belle and Liv

## You'll Need:

- 2 cups sushi rice (short- or medium-grain white rice), cooked according to the package directions
- 1/2 packet (5.29 ounces) sushi rice seasoning powder
- 1 package (5.82 ounces) fried tofu skin pouches (inari) refrigerated or canned (10 ounces)
- Soy sauce for dipping
- Pickled ginger for serving

## Equipment:

- Measuring cups and spoons
- Medium bowl (about 3 quarts)
- Rubber spatula
- Medium plate
- Soup spoon

 # Instant Inari Sushi

{Makes 8 stuffed pouches}

**1.** Put the rice in a medium-sized bowl.

**2.** Pour in the seasoning powder and mix it up really well. The skins are usually packed in a sweet sauce, so if you can't find the seasoning powder, use this sauce to season your rice.

**3.** Open the package of inari and be careful taking the little envelopes out because they can tear. Look for the open side of the envelope then slide your finger into it to open up the pouch.

**4.** Spoon the rice mixture into the envelopes and gently pack in the rice until it looks like a little pillow.

**5.** Serve with soy sauce and pickled ginger.

*Add seasoning to warm rice.*

*Carefully stuff the tofu envelopes.*

*Arrange on a plate.*

*Carefully cut pitted avocado.*

## You'll Need:

- 1 tablespoon finely **chopped** garlic
- 2 tablespoons finely chopped white onion
- 1 tablespoon finely chopped fresh jalapeño chile pepper
- 1 large ripe avocado (the Haas variety is the best)
- 1 teaspoon freshly squeezed lime juice
- Dash of salt
- 1 tablespoon chopped ripe tomato
- 1 tablespoon chopped fresh cilantro
- Tortillas or corn chips for serving

## Equipment:

- Measuring cups and spoons
- Medium bowl (about 3 quarts)
- Large wooden spoon for stirring
- Butter knife

*Put avocado in bowl.*

 # Chef Jorge's Guacamole

{Makes 1-1/2 cups guacamole }

1. Put the garlic, onion, and jalapeño in the bowl and use the wooden spoon to stir them together.

2. Have an adult help cut the avocado vertically in half, from the narrow end to the wide end; remove the large seed or pit.

3. Hold one avocado half in your hand and use the butter knife to cut through the flesh of the avocado into long strips, making sure not to cut through the skin. Cut the avocado flesh in the other direction to make cubes. Turn the avocado inside out, then drop the cubes into the bowl with the garlic-onion mixture. Repeat with the other avocado half.

4. Add the lime juice to the bowl. Mash the avocado with the wooden spoon until it's creamy but still a little lumpy. Add the salt, chopped tomato, and cilantro and mix to combine.

5. Serve the guacamole with tortilla or corn chips, or use it in tacos.

*Add tomato, onion, and cilantro.*

"Our friend Chef Jorge uses a *molcajete*—the bowl-like thing called a mortar in English—and a *tejolote*—the round-bottomed rock used for grinding known in English as a pestle. They are both made of volcanic rock but you can use a bowl and wooden spoon instead."—Belle

**Bake** When you bake things, you cook them with dry heat at a set temperature for a set amount of time. But baking is more than that. Baking changes things on a molecular level—molecules are the strings of atoms that make up everything. The dry heat allows gas bubbles to form in cake batter or bread dough so they rise (increase in volume and get puffier).

**Baste** Basting means that liquid is poured over the surface of what you're cooking. You can use a spoon, a basting bulb, or a basting brush. What you're doing is keeping the food from drying out and helping to produce that golden brown roasted color. You can baste a turkey or chicken or other meats with the juices that settle in the bottom of the roasting pan. You can also baste things with melted butter, orange juice, or marinade, for example.

**Beat** When you beat eggs or batter, you're actually hitting them with a flat surface of some kind. That surface can be the blades of a fork, a whisk, a spatula, or the small flat surfaces on the blades of your hand mixer. What you're doing is forcing little air bubbles into a liquid. When heat is applied, these air bubbles expand and make whatever you're cooking lighter and fluffier.

**Boil** As you know, high heat will cause liquids to boil. Water boils at 212°F (100°C). The surface of the liquid gets all bubbly and steam rises off it because the heat is making the molecules of water rush around faster and faster until they turn to vapor. You can use all that energy to cook stuff pretty fast. Other things, such as sugar syrup, can also boil, and they can get much hotter than water. So pay attention to all our cautions in the recipes.

**Brown** Browning actually changes the color of whatever you're cooking to brown. It's usually done in a hot skillet or frying pan with a little oil, butter, or some other kind of fat. The heat in the pan causes the outside surface of the meat, potato, spaghetti, or whatever else to get a crispy brown crust. For meat, browning helps seal in the flavors.

You can also brown butter. That means heating butter until it starts to turn golden brown. As soon as the butter shows a little brown in the bubbles at the edges of the pan, remove the pan from the heat, because butter will go from nutty, yummy brown to burned and black before you know it.

Oil and butter get hotter than boiling water, and you know how very hot that is! So get some adult help when you are going to brown something.

**Butter or grease; butter and flour** If you're asked to butter or grease a pan, it means to apply a thin coating of butter, margarine, shortening, vegetable oil, or nonstick vegetable cooking spray to the inside surfaces of an unheated pan or pot. Sometimes you're asked to butter and flour a pan or mold.

First, you spread butter evenly over the inside of the pan using your fingers or a piece of paper towel. Then you sprinkle a couple tablespoons of flour into the pan and tip the pan to one side and then the other until the greased insides of the pan have a thin layer of flour sticking to them. We butter or butter and flour pans because the greasy layer keeps the food we're cooking or baking from sticking to the pan, so it's easier to get the food out when we are done—and it helps in cleanup, too.

**Chop** To chop things, cut them into various-sized pieces. Coarsely chopped means "biggish pieces" and finely chopped means "smallish pieces." A coarsely chopped onion is one with pieces about 1/2-inch square; a finely chopped one is cut in pieces about 1/4-inch square or smaller.

**Cream** You'll see the word cream used when mixing together butter and sugar. You can stir soft butter and sugar, but creaming means you beat the two together until the texture of the sugar isn't gritty anymore. Creamed sugar is light yellow and fluffy; the changed consistency actually affects the texture of a finished cookie or cake.

**Dice** Dicing is cutting vegetables, cheese, or meat into little squares or cubes . . . well, kind of like small dice.

**Fold** When you have a light airy mixture such as beaten egg whites and you want to combine it with dry ingredients such as flour or cocoa, a recipe will ask you to "fold" the dry ingredients in. You don't want to stir or mix because that would break up the delicate little air bubbles you worked so hard to trap in the beaten egg whites.

Add a little of your dry ingredients to the bowl of the beaten whites and then use your spatula to lift one side of the egg whites and gently fold it over the top of the rest of the ingredients. Then you do the same from the other side. Do this once more, and then sprinkle in a little more dry stuff. Repeat until all your dry ingredients have been "folded" into the egg whites and you have a smooth but fluffy batter.

**Garnish** To garnish means "to decorate." You could just arrange things on a plate in a pleasing way, but garnishing gives your plate a little something special. A sprig of fresh parsley tucked in between the potatoes and the meat gives a little extra eye appeal. A garnish can be a few thin slices of green apple laid on the side of the plate or maybe some chopped pecans or sliced almonds sprinkled over the top of your dish. It's a small thing that catches your eye and sparks your imagination.

**Knead** When you knead bread dough, you fold the ball of dough once, then push the dough back into a solid mass again, using the heels of your hands. What you're doing is transforming the molecules inside the dough. The gluten (a protein) in the flour is rearranging itself into long strings that will give bread the elasticity (stretchability) it needs to rise.

**Marinate** Marinating is a fancy term for "soaking." You marinate meat, fish, vegetables, or cheese in a liquid called a marinade before you cook it. This step gives food more flavor, moisture, and tenderness when it is finally cooked.

Marinades have at least one ingredient that will make your mouth pucker, such as lemon juice, vinegar, wine, fruit juice, or buttermilk. These slightly acidic ingredients help the marinade soak through the surface of the food.

**Microwave** Microwaves are similar to radio waves and they are used in a microwave oven to shake up the molecules inside food of any kind. Those molecules absorb the energy from the microwaves and start to dance around faster and faster and transfer their energy into the food in the oven. Okay, so they don't really dance, but you get the picture. The "dancing" is what cooks your food—from the inside out.

**Puree** To puree means to break food into itsy-bitsy pieces. You can use a mortar and pestle or a food mill but we usually do it in a food processor or a blender. For example, you can puree soups—turning broth and chunks of vegetables into a thick soup with a smooth consistency and color. Here's how it works: instead of the liquid flowing easily around the hunks of carrots or squash, you have lots of tiny bits of the vegetable suspended in the liquid. This makes the liquid move a lot slower, so it becomes thick.

## Roast
You can roast on a spit over a barbecue or over a campfire like in cowboy movies. But most people roast in the oven. Roasting works just like baking (cooking in dry heat) only it's done to meat, fish, and vegetables. Roast chicken, roast beef, and roasted potatoes are just a few examples of roasted food that we love.

## Sauté
To sauté, first you warm a little oil or butter in a skillet or frying pan over medium heat. Then you add cut-up vegetables or meat and move them around in the pan so they don't stick or burn. The medium heat lets the ingredients cook kind of slow. If you use a lot more oil and turn up the heat, you'll find yourself frying. If you use too little oil, the food will stick and burn.

## Scald
We've heard only of scalding milk in recipes. To do this, heat the milk to the point that it almost boils. When you see small bubbles popping up around the edges of the pan, and a skin-like layer starts to form on top of the milk in the pan, turn the heat off and take the pan off the burner. Remove the "skin" before using scalded milk in your recipe.

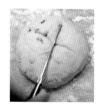

## Score
Scoring means "to cut through the surface or edges of something just deep enough to expose a little of the inside." You can score the top of bread dough so the bread can expand, or you can score meat so that marinades and seasonings will penetrate deeper.

## Sift
Sifting removes the lumps from dry ingredients such as flour or confectioners' (powdered) sugar. It also puts a little air in between the particles so things turn out lighter and fluffier. We do it a lot in baking.

## Simmer
Often you will be asked to bring ingredients to a boil and then lower the heat to a simmer. When you boil, there will be bubbles breaking out all over the surface of the food, especially liquids. When you simmer, there will be less energy transferred from the heat to the liquid, so on the surface you'll see little bumps and swells instead of lots of bubbles.

## Steam
When water molecules get to bouncing faster and faster in boiling water, they eventually break the surface and shoot out into the air. You could say they are supercharged. To harness this energy for cooking, put a perforated basket or steamer just above the water level in a pot or pan. Place the ingredients evenly on the steamer, cover the pot with a tight lid, and your food cooks very fast. Veggies are especially good steamed because they stay crispy.

But be careful! Steam is a lot hotter than boiling water!

## Whisk
Whisking, like beating, forces tiny air bubbles into a liquid. A whisk is a bundle of loops made of wire or silicon held together with a handle. A brisk wrist motion sets those loops flying through a liquid, whipping and raising a foam throughout.

# INDEX